Contents

The text is recorded in full.

| n. track | These symbols indicate the beginning and end of the passages |
| end | linked to the listening activities. |

A portrait of **William Shakespeare** by an unknown artist. It is a copy made in the early 19th century of a portrait that was in the Folio edition of the plays of Shakespeare, which was published in 1623. This copy is called the **Flowers portrait** because it was owned by a family called Flowers.

The Life of
William Shakespeare

William Shakespeare was born in 1564 in Stratford-upon-Avon, a small town in central England. The exact date of his birth is not known, but many people like to believe that he was born on 23 April. This is St George's Day, the day of the patron saint of England.

William Shakespeare's father made and sold gloves. [1] He was involved in local politics in Stratford-upon-Avon, and became the town mayor. [2] It is likely that William Shakespeare was educated at the grammar school in Stratford-upon-Avon, where boys were taught Latin and Roman history.

When he was eighteen Shakespeare married Anne Hathaway, who was eight years older than himself. They had three children: a daughter, Susanna, and twins, Hamnet and Judith. Hamnet died young, at the age of eleven.

We do not know what Shakespeare did immediately after marriage, and there are a lot of stories about what have been called the 'missing years'. It is known,

1. **gloves** : you wear these on your hands.
2. **mayor** [meər] : the head of the government of a town or city.

William Shakespeare

Macbeth

Adaptation by **James Butler and Maria Lucia de Vanna**
Activities by **Bruce Hodges**
Illustrated by **Gianni De Conno**

Editors: Michela Bruzzo, Robert Hill
Design and art direction: Nadia Maestri
Computer graphics: Simona Corniola
Picture research: Laura Lagomarsino

DEALINK, DEAFLIX are trademarks licensed by
De Agostini SpA

Picture Credits
From the RSC Collection with the permission of the Governors
of the Royal Shakespeare Company: 4;
www.visitlondon.com: 5; REPUBLIC PICTURES / Album: 7;
Aquarius Collection: 8; De Agostini Picture Library: 17, 75
centre top; Corpus Christi College, Cambridge: 27; by courtesy
of the National Portrait Gallery, London: 28; Private Collection,
The Stapleton Collection / The Bridgeman Art Library: 66;
TopFoto / Woodmansterne TopFoto.co.uk: 69 bottom; © Ali
Haider / epa / Corbis: 75 top left; © Alain Nogues / Sygma /
Corbis: 75 bottom left; © Anna
Clopet / Corbis: 75 centre bottom; © Tomek Surdel / Alamy: 75
bottom right.

We would be happy to receive your comments and
suggestions, and give you any other information concerning
our material.
info@blackcat-cideb.com
blackcat-cideb.com

Printed in Italy by Litoprint, Genoa

however, that he later went to London, where he became one of the owners of a theatrical company called the Lord Chamberlain's [1] Men. It seems he was an actor before he began to write plays. He wrote thirty-eight plays, as well as poetry. After his death, some friends of Shakespeare collected his work and published it in 1623.

In 1599, Shakespeare's company built one of the most famous theatres in London, the Globe Theatre. The company changed its name to the King's Men in 1603, when James I became king, and from 1609 its main theatre was the Blackfriars.

Shakespeare became rich and successful and retired to Stratford-upon-Avon in 1613. He died there on 23 April 1616.

Visitors to Stratford-upon-Avon today can see many of the buildings associated with Shakespeare's life, including the house where he was born and Anne Hathaway's cottage. They can also visit the Royal Shakespeare Theatre and go to performances of Shakespeare's plays.

The modern reconstruction of the **Globe Theatre** in London,
very near the site of Shakespeare's Globe, which was destroyed by fire in 1613.

1. **Lord Chamberlain** : a very important official at the royal court.

Answer the questions.

1 Why do people like to think that Shakespeare was born on 23 April?
2 What kind of school did Shakespeare go to?
3 What are the 'missing years'?
4 Where did Shakespeare work when he went to London?
5 What did Shakespeare do before he started writing plays?
6 How many plays did Shakespeare write?
7 Who were the King's Men?
8 When and where did Shakespeare die?

INTERNET PROJECT

Present a more detailed report about some part of Shakespeare's life :
▶ childhood ▶ school ▶ marriage
▶ early plays, mature plays and last plays ▶ retirement

To find out about his life go to the Internet and go to www.blackcat-cideb.com or www.cideb.it. Insert the title or part of the title of the book into our search engine. Open the page to *Macbeth.* Click on the Internet project link. Scroll down the page until you find the title of this book and click on the relevant link for this project.

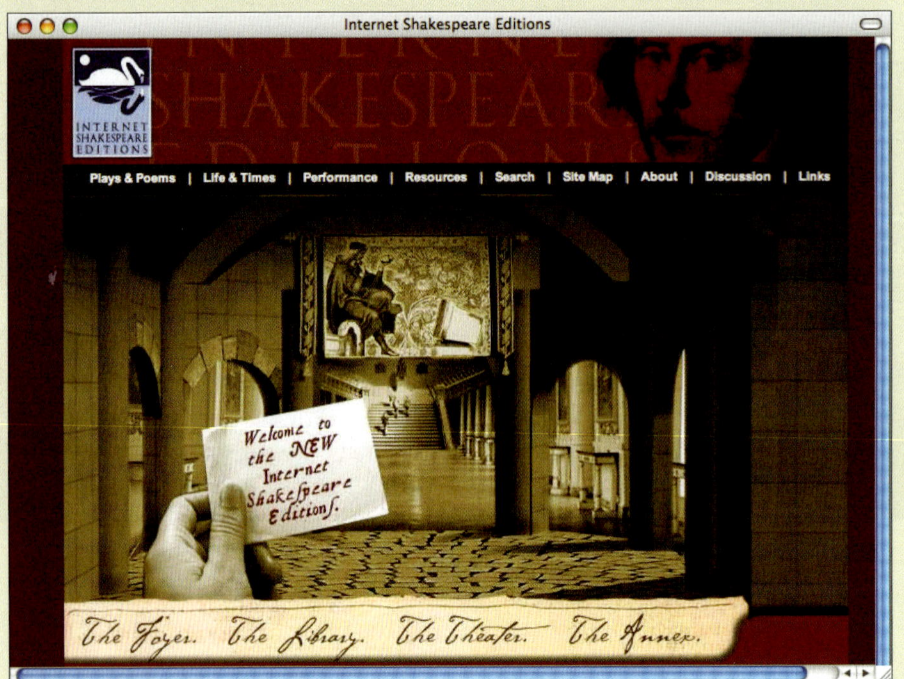

Films of Macbeth

Many film directors have been attracted to Shakespeare's tragic story of the rise and fall of the ambitious 11th-century Scottish warrior Macbeth. In fact, there are to date a total of 51 films: 32 made for the big screen, 16 made for television, two for video release and one television series.

Below are four interesting film versions of the Scottish play.

Macbeth (1948) directed by Orson Welles

This starred Orson Welles as Macbeth and Jeanette Nolan as Lady Macbeth. Welles was so keen to make the film that he agreed to shoot it in only 23 days in a B-movie studio which was normally used for cowboy films. Despite the obvious limitations of the film because of its minimal budget, many critics have admired its surrealistic qualities. Welles also eliminated large parts of the play and even added a new character.

Macbeth, played by **Orson Welles**, has just seen the ghost of Banquo.

King Duncan (right) and some of his thanes, from the film directed by **Roman Polanski**.

Macbeth (1971) directed by Roman Polanski

Starring Jon Finch and Francesca Annis, this was Polanski's first film project after the horrifying murder of his pregnant wife Sharon Tate, and perhaps this personal tragedy helps explain the brutality and cruelty which appears throughout the film. Additional scenes that are not shown in Shakespeare's play were added, such as the execution of the Thane of Cawdor and the murder of Duncan. Also, some dramatic soliloquies are presented as voice-overs to make them seem more realistic. Some critics complained about the violence of the film, but others praised it as an original interpretation of Shakespeare's tragedy.

Scotland, Pa **(2002) directed by Billy Morrissette**

Morrissette moved *Macbeth* from the 11th century to the 20th century, and from Scotland, the nation, to Scotland, a small town in Pennsylvania (the 'Pa' of the title). Macbeth and his wife now work in a fast food restaurant called 'Duncan's Café'. The story of this film is certainly based on the original tragedy, but the result is a dark comedy. However, Shakespeare's original language can be heard sometimes in this film – in the background coming out of a radio.

Macbeth **(2006) by Geoffrey Wright**

Australian director Geoffrey Wright also updated Macbeth. He set his version in present-day Melbourne, Australia. Macbeth works for a gangland boss named Duncan. The actors all speak with Australian accents. The violence is as vivid as any other film about criminal gangs. However, the words spoken are mostly those composed by Shakespeare himself. The director says he chose this play because the characters have very strong motivations for their actions. He also liked the ideas about evil in the play. 'I wonder,' he said, 'if evil knows it's evil, or whether it thinks, "We're just fighting for what we believe in."'

1 Comprehension check

For questions 1-10, choose from the films (A-D). There is an example at the beginning.

A	Orson Welles's *Macbeth*	**C**	Roman Polanski's *Macbeth*
B	Billy Morrissette's *Macbeth*	**D**	Geoffrey Wright's *Macbeth*

Which film(s)

has additional scenes added to it?	0	B
has the director also playing the main role?	1	....
is not a tragedy?	2	....
has actors speaking in an Australian accent?	3	....
seems to reflect the life of the director?	4	....
are in a 'modern' setting?	5 .... 6	
was made with very little money?	7	....
has a criminal setting?	8	....
has very little scenery and props?	9	....
was filmed in a studio where westerns were normally made?	10	....

The Scotland of Mac Bethad, (the real Macbeth), the Lord of Moray

Here is a map of Scotland in around 1100, the time when the real King Macbeth (1005-1057) lived. The real Macbeth lived at a time when the Scottish rulers in the south established strong contacts with the Norman-French rulers of England in Northumbria. Macbeth himself began as the Lord of Moray in the north. Also, notice that Gaelic was the main language; English was spoken in Northumbria on the border, and Norse, the language of the Vikings, who began invading Scotland in the late 8th century, in the north.

The Characters

Duncan	King of Scotland
Malcolm }	
Donalbain }	his sons
Macbeth	Thane of Glamis, later of Cawdor, later King of Scotland
Banquo	Friend of Macbeth
Macduff }	
Lennox }	Thanes of Scotland
Ross }	
Lady Macbeth	Wife of Macbeth
Fleance	Banquo's son
Seyward	Earl of Northumberland
Porter of Macbeth's castle	
Doctor	
Young Seyward	
Three witches	
Hecate	goddess of the witches

Before you read

1 Listening

track 02

FCE

You will hear about Macbeth's victory against his king's enemies and Macbeth's strange meeting with some witches.
(You will hear the word 'thane', which is the old Scottish word for 'lord'. So, the Thane of Cawdor is the Lord of Cawdor.)

1 At the beginning of his war against the King of Scotland, the Thane of Cawdor

   A ☐ lost many battles.

   B ☐ won many battles.

   C ☐ was more or less equal to the King of Scotland.

2 The Thane of Cawdor was helped by

   A ☐ the Thane of Glamis.

   B ☐ the King of Norway.

   C ☐ most of Duncan's thanes.

3 Duncan, the King of Scotland, wanted to make Macbeth the new Thane of Cawdor because

   A ☐ Macbeth had done so much for him in the war.

   B ☐ the old Thane of Cawdor had died in the war.

   C ☐ Macbeth had asked to become the Thane of Cawdor.

4 At first, Banquo and Macbeth thought that the strange figures could be men because

   A ☐ they could not see them well.

   B ☐ they did not dress like women.

   C ☐ they had beards.

5 Banquo thought that the witches called Macbeth the Thane of Cawdor because

   A ☐ they were confused.

   B ☐ they had talked with Duncan.

   C ☐ they were predicting the future.

6 Macbeth believed the witches when he heard that

   A ☐ Banquo was the new Thane of Cawdor.

   B ☐ Banquo's children would be kings of Scotland.

   C ☐ he was the new Thane of Cawdor.

PART ONE

Macbeth and the Witches

Duncan, the King of Scotland, was a good king, who was liked by most of his lords, or thanes. The Thane of Cawdor, however, wanted to kill Duncan and become king. He asked the King of Norway to come to Scotland with a great army.

At first everything went well for the King of Norway and the Thane of Cawdor. Their army was strong, and they had some victories against the Scottish.

Then King Duncan's army fought against the army of the King of Norway and the Thane of Cawdor. There was a desperate battle to save Scotland. One of Duncan's loyal thanes was called Macbeth. He was Thane of Glamis. [1] Macbeth fought very hard in the battle against the Thane of Cawdor, and he defeated the enemy. Duncan was very pleased with Macbeth, and wanted to reward [2] him for his loyalty. He called one of his Thanes.

1. **Glamis** : pronunciation [glamz].
2. **reward** : something given in return for service or merit.

'Ross,' Duncan said, 'I want you to do something for me. I have decided to execute [1] the Thane of Cawdor because he is a rebel who tried to kill me and become king. I want you to go to Macbeth and to tell him that he will be the new Thane of Cawdor. It is my reward to him for his courage and loyalty.'

'Yes, sir,' said Ross. 'I'll go immediately and tell Macbeth.'

Macbeth and his friend, Banquo, were both tired after the battle. They were walking together, and they were talking about the events of the day. They were both excited and pleased that Duncan had won the battle. Suddenly Banquo stopped.

'Look!' he cried. 'Look at them!'

Macbeth looked, and saw in front of them three very strange figures. It was difficult to tell if they were men or women. They looked like old women, but they had beards and they were very ugly. They were standing around a fire, and there was a cooking-pot on it. There was a horrible smell coming from the cooking-pot.

'Are you women, or are you spirits?' Banquo asked them.

'Answer him,' Macbeth said. 'Are you women or are you spirits?'

The first witch looked at Macbeth, and said,

'Welcome Macbeth, Thane of Glamis.'

The second witch looked at Macbeth, and said,

'Welcome, Macbeth, Thane of Cawdor.'

The third witch looked at Macbeth, and said to him,

'Welcome, Macbeth, King of Scotland.'

Macbeth was very surprised at what the three witches had told him, and he did not say anything. Banquo then asked the witches a question.

'You tell my friend that he will be Thane of Cawdor, and then King of Scotland, but you say nothing to me. If you can really see into the future, tell us something about my future. What will happen to me?'

One of the witches replied,

'You will be less than Macbeth, but more than Macbeth.'

The second witch told him,

'You will be less lucky than Macbeth, but you will be more lucky.'

1. **execute** : kill as a punishment.

The third witch told Banquo,

'You will never be king, but your children's children will be kings.'

After making these predictions, the witches suddenly disappeared.

'It's very strange!' Macbeth said to Banquo. 'They say that I will be Thane of Cawdor, and then king — and your children's children will be kings! I don't believe it, though. I don't know who they are, or what they are, but what they say makes no sense.'

'I don't know what to think,' said Banquo. 'Perhaps — '

Just as Banquo was speaking, Ross appeared.

'I have come from King Duncan,' he told Macbeth. 'I have a message for you from the king. He wants to reward you because he is very pleased with your courage and loyalty. He gave me a message to bring to you. You are the new Thane of Cawdor.'

Macbeth and Banquo looked at each other in astonishment. [1]

'The witches told the truth!' Macbeth said to Banquo.

'Be careful, my friend,' Banquo replied. 'They also told you that you'd be king, but perhaps the witches were bad spirits. I have heard that such spirits try to make men do wicked [2] things by making them promises.'

Macbeth said nothing to his friend, but he could not stop thinking about what the witches had said. He had always been loyal to Duncan, but now he began to question his loyalty for the first time. 'The witches told the truth,' he thought. 'They said I would be Thane of Cawdor, and now I am Thane of Cawdor. Perhaps I'll also be king one day!' He was excited about the idea of becoming king, but he was also frightened. 'I want to be king,' he thought, 'but Duncan is my friend — I don't want to hurt him.'

---

1. **astonishment** : great surprise.   2. **wicked** [wɪkɪd] : bad.

The text and **beyond**

1 Comprehension check

Answer the following questions.

1 Why did the King of Norway fight against Duncan?
2 How did Macbeth feel after the battle?
3 Why was the king pleased with Macbeth?
4 How did Duncan reward Macbeth?
5 Describe the three witches.
6 What did the three witches tell Macbeth and Banquo?
7 What advice did Banquo give Macbeth about the witches?
8 What did Macbeth think about the witches?
9 Why were Macbeth and Banquo so astonished at Ross's message?

2 Discussion

What do you think the witches mean when they say 'You will be less lucky than Macbeth, but you will be more lucky.'? (bottom of page 13).

3 Speaking: some good advice

You are a good friend of Macbeth's, and your partner is Macbeth. Discuss what Macbeth should do after hearing the predictions of the witches. Explain your choices. The person playing Macbeth should also explain why he/she will follow or not follow the friend's advice.

A He should do nothing.
B He should begin planning to become king.
C He should wait and see what Banquo will do after hearing the prediction.
D *Your idea: ...*

FCE **4** A weird fate

For questions 1-7, read the text below and decide which answer (A, B, C or D) best fits each space. There is an example at the beginning (0).

In the original *Macbeth*, Shakespeare called the witches the 'weird sisters'. Nowadays, when (0) .A... English speakers hear about 'weird sisters', they probably (1) .... that these sisters are strange, maybe supernatural and that they might (2) .... you an uneasy feeling. But in Shakespeare's time the word 'weird' was connected with 'fate' and 'destiny'. In fact, the section on the life of Macbeth in Raphael Holinshed's *Chronicles* (1577), an early English history book (3) ...... was Shakespeare's source for his play, presents the weird sisters (4) .... goddesses of fate. In Nordic mythology these goddesses of fate were called Norns. Three important (**5**) .... keep alive Ygdrasil — the Tree of Existence. One of these Norns governs the past, another the present and another the future. There are (**6**) .... other Norns — one of these goddesses governs the life of every person according to Nordic mythology.

Shakespeare, though, combined Nordic Norns, witches and classical goddesses of the underworld to make his weird sisters. In the end, the new meaning of 'weird' first (**7**) .... in Shakespeare's *Macbeth*.

The three witches as painted by the Swiss Romantic painter Johann Heinrich Füssli (1741-1825).

0 Ⓐ native	**B** born	**C** natural	**D** resident
1 **A** consider	**B** judge	**C** think	**D** regard
2 **A** offer	**B** bring	**C** take	**D** give
3 **A** what	**B** who	**C** that	**D** whose
4 **A** like	**B** similar	**C** as	**D** for
5 **A** individuals	**B** ones	**C** others	**D** singles
6 **A** lots	**B** plenty	**C** many	**D** number
7 **A** comes	**B** arrives	**C** shows	**D** appears

5 **Listening**

track 03

You will hear two short extracts from the original Shakespeare's play. However, before you listen, read them and try to fill in the gaps with the words from the box. Then listen and check your answers.

Speak	Thane	greater	happier	Cawdor	Banquo	king	Hail

Extract One

Macbeth (*to the witches*)**:** Speak if you can! What are you?

First Witch: All hail,[1] Macbeth! Hail to thee,[2] (**1**)..................... of Glamis!

Second Witch: All hail, Macbeth. Hail to thee, Thane of (**2**)..................... !

Third Witch: All hail, Macbeth, that shalt be (**3**)..................... hereafter![3]

1. **hail** : welcome.
2. **thee** : you.

3. **hereafter** : after this time.

Extract Two

Banquo: (4)..................... then to me, who neither beg [1] nor fear

Your favours, [2] nor your hate.

First Witch: Hail!

Second Witch: Hail!

Third Witch: (5)..................... !

First Witch: Lesser than Macbeth, and (6)..................... .

Second Witch: Not so happy, yet much (7)..................... .

Third Witch: Thou [3] shalt get [4] kings, though thou be none.

So all hail, Macbeth, and (8)..................... !

Now, using a dictionary, rewrite Extract One in modern English.

6 Writing

Imagine you are Banquo. Read this part of a letter from a friend. Write a letter in 120-180 words in an appropriate style.

Tell me about your meeting with the witches.
What were they like?
Did they tell you anything about the future?

7 Speaking: the future today

In Shakespeare's time some people were convinced that witches existed and had the power to see the future. With your partner prepare a short report on how people predict the future today. Use the list of ways of predicting the future and the following questions to help you.

Which of the following do you believe in?
Which don't you believe in?
Which ones do people in your society believe in?
Which ones are the most popular?

Ways of predicting the future

- weather reports
- reading tea leaves
- reading palms
- opinion polls for elections
- astrology
- tarot cards
- statistics
- *any others?*

1. **beg** : ask.
2. **favours** : good services.
3. **thou** : old-fashioned, poetic, or religious word for 'you'.
4. **get** : (old-fashioned use), be the father of.

The Murder of the King

1   **After the battle, King Duncan decided to go on a journey around Scotland. He told Macbeth that he would go and stay in his castle.**

'I will be very happy to be your host, Sir,' Macbeth told him. 'I will write to my wife so that she can prepare everything for us.'

Macbeth wrote a long letter to his wife. He told her that the king was coming to stay in the castle, and he asked her to prepare everything for the visit. He also told her about the encounter with the three witches, and what they had said about the future.

2   Lady Macbeth read her husband's letter with great interest and excitement. 'Thane of Cawdor, and then king,' she thought. 'But I know you, husband,' she said to herself. 'You want to be king — but you don't want to do anything wicked to become king. Your nature is too gentle to be really ambitious. This is a great opportunity for us. Hurry home, my love, and I'll teach you to be cruel for the sake of [1] your ambition. I'll put courage into you!'

When Macbeth and the king arrived at the castle, Lady Macbeth had already made a plan. She told her husband that he had to act very cheerfully and innocently — and that she had made a plan to make him king.

---

1. **for the sake of** : in the interest of.

(3) 'Leave everything to me,' she said. 'Duncan will never leave the castle alive!'

Macbeth listened to his wife. 'It's true,' he thought, 'I want to be king — but I don't want to kill Duncan — I'm frightened! He's my king, and my guest here in the castle. To murder him would be a terrible crime!'

He argued with Lady Macbeth.

'We cannot kill the king,' he told her. 'He has been a good friend to me, and I can't murder him.'

Lady Macbeth was very angry with her husband.

'Why did you tell me about the three witches?' she demanded angrily.
(4) 'They called you "king", didn't they? Be brave, and you can have the throne!'

'But if we fail?' Macbeth asked her. 'What happens to us if we fail?'

'Don't worry about that,' his wife said. 'We won't fail. I have a plan. Duncan's room is guarded by two soldiers. I'll make sure that the soldiers are given a lot of wine tonight, and I'll put something in the wine to make them sleep very heavily. They won't know what's happening. You'll be able to walk past them and into the king's room without anyone seeing you. Then you can kill Duncan, and we'll blame the soldiers [1] for the murder.'

'You're right!' Macbeth said excitedly. 'If the king is killed with the soldiers' knives, everyone will think they're guilty.'

'Exactly,' Lady Macbeth said. 'Who would dare [2] to say that you and I
(5) knew anything about it? People might suspect us, but they could never say anything.'

Late that night Macbeth was alone in the castle. He was thinking about the murder when suddenly he saw a knife in front of him. The knife was red with blood. He was very frightened. When he looked again, the knife had gone.

'It was just my imagination,' he told himself. 'There was nothing there at
(6) all.' He shuddered [3] with fear. 'I must be brave,' he told himself. 'If I want to be king, I must be brave.'

He went very quietly to the room of the two soldiers. They were fast asleep, [4] and the room smelt of wine. He took a knife from one of the

---

1. **blame the soldiers** : say they are responsible.
2. **dare** : have the courage.
3. **shuddered** : shook, trembled.
4. **fast asleep** : sleeping deeply.

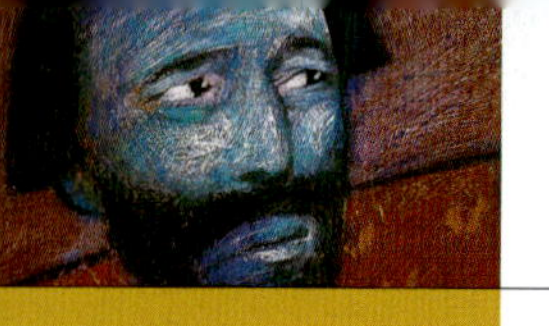

soldiers, and went into the king's bedroom. The king was asleep. Macbeth killed him with the soldier's knife.

Lady Macbeth saw her husband when he came back out of the soldiers' room.

'Well?' she asked him. 'Did you do it?'

Macbeth was very pale.

'Duncan is dead,' he told her. 'It's a terrible thing I've done. Afterwards, I heard a voice. It said, "There will be no more sleep. Macbeth has murdered sleep." It was a frightening voice.'

Lady Macbeth looked at him. Even she was frightened for a moment.

'Did it say anything else?' she asked.

'The voice was very loud,' Macbeth said. 'It cried out, "Macbeth has murdered sleep — Macbeth will never sleep again". I thought everyone in the castle would hear the voice.'

'You're like a child!' Lady Macbeth told him angrily. 'There was no voice, it was only your own fear which you heard. Go and wash the blood from your hands.' Then she noticed the knife in Macbeth's hand.

'But the knife, why are you carrying the knife? You should have left it with the soldiers! Take it back.'

'I can't go back in there,' Macbeth said. 'I'll never go back in there!'

'Give me the knife,' Lady Macbeth ordered. 'I'm not afraid to go in there.'

7   Lady Macbeth took the knife, and went into the soldiers' room. They were still sleeping. She covered the soldiers with the king's blood, and left the knife in their room. When she came out of the room, she saw that Macbeth was looking at his hands. They were red with blood.

'I'll never be able to wash the blood away,' he said sadly. 'I have done a terrible thing.'

'Look at my hands,' Lady Macbeth told him scornfully.[1] 'They're red like yours — but I'm not afraid like you! A little water will remove the traces of our crime.'

Suddenly they heard a noise at the castle gate. Someone wanted to come in.

'Quickly!' Lady Macbeth commanded. 'We'll go back into our own room — no one must know we've been awake tonight.'

The knocking at the castle gate continued.

---

1. **scornfully** : with contempt.

The text and **beyond**

1 Comprehension check

Answer the following questions.

1   What did King Duncan decide to do after the battle?
2   What did Macbeth tell his wife in his letter?
3   In Lady Macbeth's opinion, why did her husband need her help?
4   How did Macbeth first react to his wife's plan to kill the king?
5   What was Lady Macbeth's plan?
6   What strange thing did Macbeth see before he killed the king?
7   Macbeth heard a voice after he killed the king. What did the voice tell him?
8   What did Lady Macbeth think the voice was?

2 Poetic sleep

In Shakespeare's original play, he gives us a complex poetic image of sleep. Read the simplified version below and then choose answers to the question. Briefly justify your answer. You can choose more than one answer.

Macbeth said, 'I thought I heard a voice that cried, "Sleep no more! Macbeth murders sleep" - innocent sleep, sleep that makes our worries seem smaller, the death of each day's life, the bath that makes us feel better after work, the medicine that calms our hurt feelings, the great food of life.'

'What do you mean?' asked Lady Macbeth.

Macbeth continued, 'Still the voice cried to the whole castle, "Sleep no more! Glamis has murdered sleep, and so Cawdor will sleep no more. Macbeth will sleep no more."'

What does 'Macbeth murders sleep' mean? Discuss in pairs or small groups.

A   Macbeth will not sleep anymore because he will feel so bad about killing the king.
B   Macbeth killed people who were sleeping and without any defence.
C   The people in the castle should sleep no more, in other words they should wake up and see the horrible thing that has happened.
D   Sleep is like a nurse who cares for the sick, a mother who feeds and takes away our worries; and Macbeth has killed her.
E   *Your idea: ...*

3 Getting the stain out

When Macbeth says, 'I'll never be able to wash the blood away' and Lady Macbeth replies 'A little water will remove the traces of our crime', what are they really talking about? Justify your choice.

A Macbeth is saying he thinks people will discover the crime easily and she disagrees.

B Macbeth is saying that he will always feel bad about his crime, and she says that she will not.

C Macbeth is saying that the amount of blood from the king is enormous; she is saying that it is not — after all as a soldier he saw much more blood.

D *Your idea: ...*

4 Speaking: a killing team

With your partner discuss the following. Present your ideas to the class.

1 Describe Macbeth and Lady Macbeth. How are they similar? How are they different?

2 Have you ever read a book or scene of a film in which a similar relationship existed between two characters who committed a crime?

5 Vocabulary – odd word out

Find the word that does not belong with the other three words and then explain why. All the words come from Parts One and Two of this book.

0 cruel / ~~ambitious~~ / wicked / evil

Ambitious is not necessarily a bad thing to be - the other three words are

1 guilty / shuddered / frightened / afraid

2 execute / crime / murder / kill

3 wicked / strange / cruel / bad

4 army / brave / battle / soldier

5 thane / king / throne / lord

6 wife / lady / children / father

7 loyal / excited / good / brave

Fill in the gaps with one of the eight 'odd words out'.

1 Macbeth was quite .... when he fought in battle but not when he had to murder his king.

2 Macbeth's wife was tired of being just .... Macbeth: she wanted to be queen.

3 The witches said that Banquo's children's children would have the .... of Scotland.

4 Killing another man in battle is not generally considered a ...., but killing one of your guests is.

5 Old women with beards standing around a pot is a .... sight.

6 Macbeth feels .... about killing his king.

7 Lady Macbeth is a very............................. person. She will stop at nothing to get what she wants.

8 Macbeth became .... when he heard the witches' prediction.

6 Listening

You will hear two short extracts from Shakespeare's original play. Listen and answer the following questions.

1 Which of the extracts comes before the murder, and which comes after the murder?

2 Listen again and put the first extract into modern English.

FCE 7 Writing

Imagine that you are Lady Macbeth. Read this part of a letter from your English-speaking friend Elizabeth. Write a letter to Elizabeth and tell her how you feel in 120-180 words in an appropriate style.

> *You must write and tell me what has happened.*
>
> *How do you feel about these events?*

T: GRADE 8

8 Speaking: the supernatural

Macbeth is filled with supernatural elements. Interestingly, in this particular play they are given rational explanations by Lady Macbeth, even if she does accept the predictions of the witches.

What do you think of supernatural things such as ghosts and witches? Present a short report explaining your opinions.

Scotland's History

The original inhabitants of Scotland were the Picts and the Scots – the Picts were people of Celtic origin, and the Scots came from Ireland. The Picts and the Scots defended Scotland against the Romans. In 120 AD the Roman Emperor Hadrian built a wall between England and Scotland to keep the Scottish out. Hadrian's Wall can still be seen today, and it is a major tourist attraction.

Scotland was converted to Christianity in the sixth century by missionaries from Ireland. In the ninth century Scotland was united under the same king for the first time, as the country struggled to fight off invasions from the Vikings.

By the tenth century the Scottish had successfully repulsed the Vikings, and so they themselves began to attack Northumbria, but without much success. Then the Scottish King Malcolm II Mackenneth defeated the Northumbrians in 1018. His grandson became his successor as Duncan I. This is the King Duncan of Shakespeare's play. His reign was not peaceful and in 1040 Duncan was killed by his general, Macbeth. Macbeth ruled until 1057, when he was defeated by Duncan's son Malcolm III Canmore. Malcolm had spent many years in exile in

Part of **Hadrian's Wall**.

The Battle of Bannockburn in June 1314, in a fifteenth-century Scottish manuscript.

England, and he eventually married an English princess. This further increased the influence of England on Scotland.

The English King Edward I invaded Scotland in the thirteenth century, and he seemed to have defeated the country. In 1314, however, the Scots rebelled against the English, and their leader, Robert Bruce, defeated the English army at the Battle of Bannockburn. After this battle England and Scotland remained separate countries for nearly three hundred years.

King James I of England, who had come to the throne as King James VI of Scotland, in a portrait painted in 1621 by Daniel Mytens.

Scotland became a Protestant country at the time of the Reformation, although the queen of Scotland, Mary Stuart, was a Roman Catholic. After the death of Elizabeth I of England, Mary Stuart's son, James VI of Scotland, became James I of England. In this way the two countries were united for the first time under the same king. The union was made final in 1707 with the Act of Union, when Scotland became part of Great Britain.

Despite the Act of Union the Highland families of Scotland opposed English rule in the 1700s. These families were known as 'clans', and each was governed by a 'clan chief'. Each clan wore a distinct tartan [1] by which it could be recognised. The clans rebelled unsuccessfully against the English in 1715 and in 1745. The English treated the rebels with great cruelty, and tried to suppress their traditional way of

1.   tartan :

life. The wearing of tartans was forbidden, as was the use of Gaelic, the traditional language.

Towards the end of the 1700s the clan chiefs realised that they could become wealthy by raising sheep for their wool. Sheep farming requires much less human labour than other kinds of farming. So, the clan chiefs needed fewer people to work the land, and began to force their own people off their Highland farms. This became known as the 'Highland clearances'. The clan chiefs destroyed the old Highland way of life, and many Highland Scots left the country to settle in America, Australia and Canada.

During the twentieth century the Scottish economy was helped by the discovery of oil in the North Sea. This discovery contributed to a revival of interest in Scottish independence. In a referendum in 1997 most Scots voted in favour of a Scottish Parliament, and in 1998 the Scottish Executive (whose official name was changed to the Scottish Government in 2007) and the Scottish Parliament were formed. Although Scotland is not independent, the Scottish Government and the Scottish Parliament now decide all the things previously decided in London.

Today Scotland has an important tourist industry. Many 'Scottish Americans', the descendants of Highlanders who left Scotland during the Highland clearances of the past, come to explore their past. It is also a popular holiday destination for people from all over the world, who come to visit Scotland's celebrated Highlands, lochs, golf courses, and sample its famous whiskies.

1 Comprehension check

Answer the following questions.

1   Where did the Scots originally come from?
2   Who were the Picts?
3   What and where is Hadrian's Wall?
4   Who was the real Macbeth?
5   How did he become king?
6   When did he rule?
7   Who was his successor?
8   What were some of the consequences of the Act of Union in 1707?
9   How did the clan chiefs destroy the old Highland life?
10   What is Scotland famous for today?

▶▶▶ **INTERNET** PROJECT ◀◀◀

Go to the Internet and go to www.blackcat-cideb.com or www.cideb.it.
Insert the title or part of the title of the book into our search engine.
Open the page to *Macbeth*. Click on the Internet project link.
Scroll down the page until you find the title of this book and click on
the relevant link for this project.

Braveheart (1995) tells the story of William Wallace, a Scottish rebel at the time
of the English invasion by Edward I in the 13th century.

Find out the answers to the following questions.

- Who was the director and star of *Braveheart*?
- What was the name of the screenwriter?
- How many Academy Awards did the film win and in which categories?
- Is the film considered historically accurate?
- How long is the film?
- Where was it made?

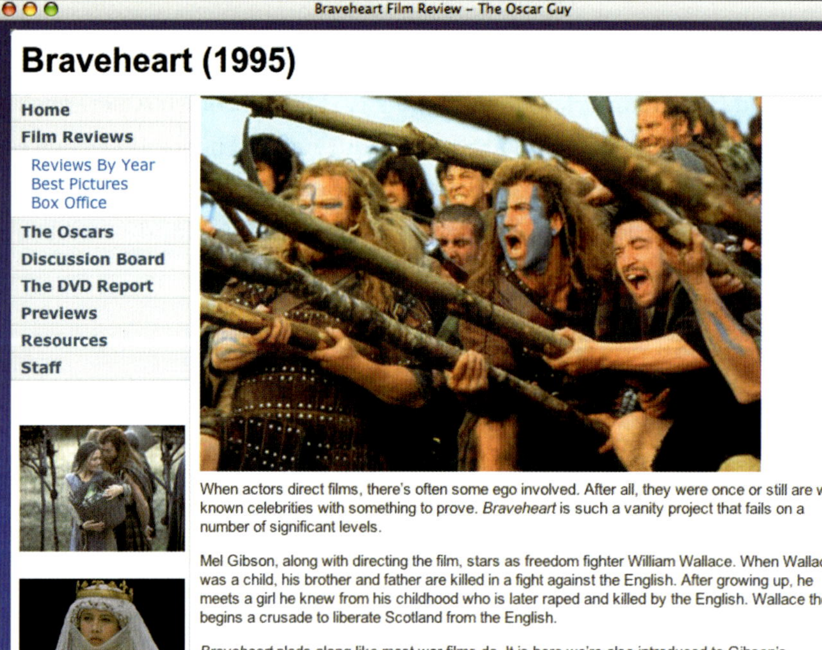

Braveheart (1995)

Home
Film Reviews
Reviews By Year
Best Pictures
Box Office
The Oscars
Discussion Board
The DVD Report
Previews
Resources
Staff

When actors direct films, there's often some ego involved. After all, they were once or still are well known celebrities with something to prove. *Braveheart* is such a vanity project that fails on a number of significant levels.

Mel Gibson, along with directing the film, stars as freedom fighter William Wallace. When Wallace was a child, his brother and father are killed in a fight against the English. After growing up, he meets a girl he knew from his childhood who is later raped and killed by the English. Wallace then begins a crusade to liberate Scotland from the English.

Braveheart plods along like most war films do. It is here we're also introduced to Gibson's penchant for blood and gore. While I have no problem with realism, what is included in this film amounts to little more than violence for violence's sake. Is there something about Gibson that drives him to such bloody topics. This was his debut film. It received the Academy Award for Best Picture against all logic. It's the most violent film ever to win such an honor and we've seen films like *Platoon* and *The Godfather* take Best Picture. Some violence is sufficient, but this film takes it to an extreme.

Macbeth, King of Scotland

The knocking on the castle gate was now very loud. The porter was very slow to open the gate. 'All right, all right, I can hear you,' he called out angrily. 'Don't be in such a hurry!' 

Two of the king's men, Macduff and Lennox, entered the castle. Macduff was annoyed with the porter because he had been slow to open the gate. He looked at him angrily.

'Did you go to bed late, my friend?' he asked. 'Perhaps you drank too much before you went to bed — is that why you were so slow to open the gate?'

'You're right, sir,' the porter admitted. 'I did drink too much before I went to bed.'

'I see we have woken Macbeth with our noise,' said Macduff. 'Good morning to you,' he said politely. 'Is the king awake yet?'

'He's still sleeping,' Macbeth said. 'Shall I wake him for you?'

'It's all right,' said Macduff. 'I'll wake him myself. He asked me to come early this morning.'

Macduff went off to wake the king, and Lennox and Macbeth stayed near the castle gate, talking.

'What a strange night it's been!' Lennox said to Macbeth. 'The wind blew

fiercely [1] all night. The chimneys in our house were blown down. Some people said they could hear horrible screams.'

'It was just bad weather,' Macbeth told him. 'It didn't mean anything.'

After a few minutes they heard a shout from the king's room. Macduff was shouting.

'Help! Help!'

'What is it? What's the matter?' cried Lennox. 'Is it the king?'

Macduff came out of the king's room. He was very pale. 'It's dreadful,' [2] he cried, 'too dreadful! Go and look for yourselves.'

'Come on,' said Macbeth, and he rushed with Lennox up to the king's room.

'Murder!' shouted Macduff. 'There's a traitor in the castle. Sound the alarm!'

People began to wake, and to come out of their rooms.

'What is it?' asked Lady Macbeth, 'Why is there such a noise?'

Macduff approached King Duncan's two sons.

'I have terrible news for you,' he told them.

'Tell us,' said Malcolm. 'Is it the king?' He looked at his brother, Donalbain.

'Yes, tell us,' said Donalbain. 'What about our father?'

Macduff looked very serious.

'I found him,' he said. 'He's been murdered!'

Macbeth and Lennox now came down from the king's room. They joined the shocked and frightened crowd of people.

'It's true,' Macbeth announced, 'Duncan has been murdered.'

'But who — !' cried Malcolm and Donalbain. 'Who would kill the king?'

'It was the two soldiers,' Lennox announced. 'When we went up there just now, we found them. They were sleeping very heavily, and they were covered with the king's blood. When we asked them questions, they looked amazed, and couldn't say anything. It was obviously them who killed the king.'

'Why did they do it?' asked Macduff. 'We must find out why they did it!'

1. **fiercely** : very strongly.
2. **dreadful** : horrible.

'We'll never know,' Macbeth said. 'I killed them straight away! I wish I hadn't been so angry.'

There was silence. Everyone looked at Macbeth for a moment.

Then Macduff spoke.

'Now we'll never know why they did it, or if someone paid them to do the murder.'

'I'm sorry,' said Macbeth. 'But when I saw them covered in the king's blood, and when I smelt the wine on their breath, I was angry — I loved the king!'

'Oh, the king, the poor king!' cried Lady Macbeth. She looked wildly [1] at everybody. 'What a terrible thing to happen here, in our house. Who could have done it?' Then she fell to the floor.

'She's fainted; the shock is too great,' Macduff said. 'Someone help her.'

Macbeth stepped forward. He picked up his wife, and carried her away.

Banquo now spoke for the first time.

'We need to plan what to do,' he said. 'I suggest we all go back to our rooms. We'll return here in one hour. Then we can decide what is to be done.'

Everyone agreed with Banquo's suggestion, and they agreed to meet in one hour.

As they were walking back to their room in the castle, Duncan's two sons spoke quietly to each other. They were shocked and frightened by their father's murder.

'Listen to me,' Donalbain said to his brother. 'I don't feel safe here. Someone has killed our father, and I don't believe Macbeth's story about the two soldiers.'

'I don't, either,' Malcolm told him. 'Why would the soldiers murder our father like that? Why would they drink wine afterwards? We'll never know what really happened now that the soldiers are dead.'

'If you want my opinion,' Donalbain said, 'Macbeth was too quick to kill them.'

Malcolm looked at him strangely. 'What do you mean?' he asked. 'What are you trying to say?'

---

1. **wildly** : in great excitement.

'Just this,' said Donalbain. 'I don't think Macbeth killed them because he was angry. I think he killed them because he didn't want us to ask them what happened. I think — '

'You suspect Macbeth of the murder?' his brother asked. 'You think he killed our father? But why would he do that?'

'I don't know,' Donalbain said. 'I think we should get away from this castle before anything happens to us. Whoever killed our father may still be here — and we may be the next to die! Let's leave Scotland, shall we?'

'I agree,' Malcolm said. 'Let's go away from here. I'll go to England. I've got friends there, and they'll help me.'

'And I'll go to Ireland,' Donalbain said. 'I'll feel safer if I'm a long way from Scotland.'

Malcolm and Donalbain left Macbeth's castle very quietly. They did not tell anyone they were going.

The others were surprised that Duncan's two sons had left the castle secretly. Suspicion fell on Donalbain and Malcolm. Macduff was the first to say what they were all beginning to think.

'It must have been Donalbain and Malcolm,' he told the others. 'I think I know what happened,' he said. 'Malcolm and Donalbain paid the two soldiers to kill Duncan because they wanted the throne for themselves. We must make sure that they suffer for this terrible crime!'

Everyone agreed with Macduff.

'Donalbain and Malcolm are murderers,' they said.

'Who will we have as our new king?' asked Macduff. 'We don't want Donalbain or Malcolm. Let's choose someone who was loyal to Duncan.'

'Let's make Macbeth the new king!' the thanes decided. 'He deserves to be king — he was Duncan's loyal friend. Remember how brave he was in the battle against the rebels and the King of Norway.'

The thanes of Scotland made Macbeth the new King of Scotland.

The text and **beyond**

1 Comprehension check

Put the events below in the correct order.

A ☐ Macbeth kills the two soldiers.

B ☐ Macduff and Lennox enter the castle.

C ☐ Macduff finds the king dead.

D ☐ Malcolm and Donalbain decide to leave the castle.

E ☐ Macduff suspects Malcolm and Donalbain of the murder.

F ☐ Macbeth and Lennox go into the king's room.

G ☐ Macduff is angry with the porter.

H ☐ Lady Macbeth falls to the floor.

2 Suspects and witnesses

1 Macbeth went to the king's room with Lennox to

  A ☐ see if the king was dead.

  B ☐ kill the two soldiers.

  C ☐ catch the murderers.

  D ☐ get his knife.

2 Malcolm and Donalbain left the castle secretly because

  A ☐ they wanted to look for their father's murderer.

  B ☐ they were afraid of their father's murderer.

  C ☐ they knew people would suspect them of the murder.

  D ☐ they wanted to look for the murder weapon.

3 Vocabulary

The following words all come from Part Three. Can you fill in the missing words in the table?

VERB	NOUN	
	ACTION	PERSON
....	....	traitor
....	crime	....
....	....	rebel
kill	....	....
murder	....	....

4 Speaking – the 'hot seat'

Read questions 1-20. Decide which ones would be appropriate to ask Lady Macbeth, which ones to ask Macbeth and which ones to ask Malcolm. The first three have been done as examples.
A chair in front of the class is the 'hot seat'. While you are sitting in this chair you are Lady Macbeth, Macbeth or Malcolm: you must answer as if you are one of those characters. Take turns sitting here. The rest of the class can ask the person in the hot seat any questions.
Here are some examples. Then think of some other questions.

1   What are you going to do to get revenge? *Malcolm*

2   Are you glad that you have followed your wife's plans? *Macbeth*

3   A good king is a representative of God on earth. What do you think about this?
    Macbeth, Lady Macbeth, Malcolm.

4   Are your plans working out well?

5   Everybody knows that a guest deserves all our protection. What do you think about this?

6   Do you think people really believe your explanation of why you killed the two soldiers?

7   What do you think of your husband's behaviour? Are you happy with it?

8   Do you think there is any connection between the weather during the night and what you did?

9   What did you first think when you heard about your father's death?

10   What was the bloody knife you saw?

11   Why didn't the witches say that your children would be kings?

12   Are you worried about Banquo and his children?

13   When did you first become frightened for the safety of you and your brother?

14   What do you think people will say about your escaping to England?

15   Will he be a good king?

16   Will she be a good queen?

17   Witches generally try to hurt humans not help them. What do you think about this?

18   Who do you think killed your father and why?

19   Did you really faint?

20   Was murder the only way for the witches' words to come true?

5 Listening

You will hear part of a conversation between Malcolm and Donalbain. For questions 1-5 complete the sentences.

Malcolm is going to ask the English king (**1**) ....

People say the king is (**2**) ....

Donalbain asks Malcolm if he thinks the king will (**3**) ....

Donalbain asks Malcolm to (**4**) ....

He says he will join Malcolm if (**5**) ....

FCE 6 Writing

Imagine you are one of the two soldiers who were guarding the king and that you managed to escape. You are now writing a letter to Malcolm and Donalbain telling them what really happened that night.
Write your letter in 120 — 180 words in an appropriate style.

7 Discussion

Talk about the following points in small groups.

- Do you think Malcolm and Donalbain have done the right thing to run away from the castle? What other alternatives did they have?
- Everybody seems to believe Macbeth's account of the events. Why do you think this is so?
- How convincing is Macbeth? Is he as convincing as Lady Macbeth?

Before you read

1 Listening

You will listen to the beginning of Part Four. For questions 1-6 complete the sentences.

1 Banquo did not like the idea that Macbeth ....

2 Macbeth thought that Banquo was dangerous because he knows about the witches and might think ....

3 Macbeth organised .... at the palace.

4 Macbeth told Banquo to bring Fleance because ....

5 Lady Macbeth didn't know about .... but she knew that Macbeth was worried about something.

6 The three men stood in front of Banquo's horse, pulled him down and ....

Banquo's Ghost

Banquo was unhappy when he remembered what the witches had promised Macbeth. 

'They said you would be Thane of Cawdor, and then King of Scotland. Everything they said has come true. Now you are the king. Perhaps it was you who killed Duncan, and not Donalbain and Malcolm!' He did not like to think that Macbeth was a murderer. 'And what was it that they promised me?' he said to himself. '"Less than Macbeth, but more than Macbeth", was that it? No, there was something else. Let me see if I can remember. Ah, yes, that was it. "You will never be king, but your children's children will be kings." I wonder what that means, and whether it will come true as well?'

Macbeth was also thinking about what the witches had said.

'They said I would be Thane of Cawdor, and then King of Scotland. Everything they said has come true. But there was something else, something about Banquo. Ah, yes, they told Banquo that his "children's children will be kings". Have I killed Duncan for nothing — will Banquo's son Fleance get the crown after me?' Macbeth thought about his old friend. 'Banquo's dangerous!' he said to himself. 'He knows about the witches — perhaps he suspects that it was me who killed Duncan. I'm afraid of him.'

Every day Macbeth's fear of Banquo and his son increased. 'I must do something,' he told himself. 'I can't live in fear all my life.' Then he thought of a wicked plan.

One day Macbeth invited all the thanes to a feast at the palace.

'Make sure that you come, my old friend,' he said to Banquo. 'The feast is in your honour.'

'I will be there,' said Banquo.

'And bring Fleance with you,' said Macbeth. 'The feast is for him as well.'

'We will be there,' said Banquo. 'We are riding out this afternoon, but we will be back at the castle for the feast.'

'Tomorrow we must have a long talk,' Macbeth went on. 'I hear that Malcolm and Donalbain have gone to England and Ireland. They are trying to make trouble for me, and we have to decide what to do about them.'

'Very well,' Banquo replied. 'Tomorrow we'll talk about that problem.'

Macbeth smiled grimly [1] to himself. 'There will be no feast for you tonight, my friend,' he thought. 'And no talk tomorrow. Tonight you and Fleance will both be dead. My men will kill you both when you are out riding. With you and Fleance dead, I will be safe.'

Lady Macbeth knew nothing of Macbeth's plan to kill Banquo and Fleance. She only knew that Macbeth was worried about something. He had been unhappy since the murder of Duncan, and was sleeping badly.

'You must forget about the murder,' she told him. 'The past is the past — we can't change it now.'

'We must be safe from danger,' Macbeth answered. 'It's true that Duncan is dead, and I am king. But still — '

'Try to be more cheerful,' [2] Lady Macbeth said. 'Remember there is the feast tonight.'

'I'll be cheerful, tonight, my love,' Macbeth promised her. 'And yet I keep thinking about Banquo and Fleance. They worry me.'

'What can we do about them?' asked his wife.

'I have already done something,' Macbeth told her. 'It's better that you don't know about it.'

Late that evening, three men were hiding near the palace.

---

1. **grimly** : seriously.
2. **cheerful** : happy in his behaviour.

'Are you sure Banquo and Fleance will come this way?' said one of the men.

'They'll come this way,' answered another.

'And when they do, we'll kill them both,' said the third man. 'Macbeth wants them both to die.'

'Here they are!' said the first man. 'I can hear the horses.'

The three men stood up, with their knives in their hands. They could see Banquo and Fleance in front of them.

'Now!' cried the third man, as he pulled Banquo off his horse. He put the knife to Banquo's heart.

'Attack!' cried the other two men. They approached Fleance.

'Ride, Fleance, ride!' shouted Banquo. 'It's a trap.'

Fleance rode away as fast as he could.

Macbeth welcomed the thanes when they arrived at the castle for the feast.

'I'm happy to see you all,' he said. He walked around the table, shaking their hands and smiling. 'Tonight we will enjoy ourselves with food and wine,' he said.

As Macbeth was walking around the table talking to his guests, he saw one of the murderers enter the room. He went up to him.

'Well?' he asked quietly. 'How did it go?'

'Banquo is dead,' the man replied.

'And Fleance?' asked Macbeth. 'Tell me that Fleance is dead as well!'

'Fleance escaped us,' the man said. 'He is free.'

'Then I'm not safe, after all. Fleance is dangerous,' Macbeth whispered. He looked at the murderer. 'You'd better go,' he ordered. 'There is blood on your face. We'll talk more tomorrow.' He sighed, and looked worried.

Lady Macbeth was looking at her husband. She knew that something was wrong.

'Tonight is a feast,' she called to him. 'The king must be cheerful tonight.'

'You're right, my love,' Macbeth told her. 'Tonight we will eat and be happy with our guests.'

'Will Your Majesty sit with us?' Lennox asked politely.

'Where shall I sit?' asked Macbeth. 'All the chairs are taken.'

'Here, Your Majesty, sit here,' said Lennox. 'There is an empty chair beside me.'

Macbeth looked at the chair beside Lennox — he saw the ghost of Banquo sitting there! Suddenly he began to tremble, and he went very pale.

'I didn't do it!' he cried out to the ghost. 'Don't sit there looking at me like that. I didn't do it!'

The ghost of Banquo looked steadily [1] at Macbeth for a moment.

'What's the matter with the king?' the thanes said. 'Why is he so

1. **steadily** : persistently, without interruption.

frightened, and who is he talking to — that chair's empty!'

'It's just an illness of his,' said Lady Macbeth. 'He's like this sometimes. He'll be all right in a moment.'

She went up to her husband.

'What's the matter with you?' she whispered angrily. 'Remember your guests. Where's your courage?'

'My courage!' responded Macbeth. 'I'm a brave man to look at that ghost and not run away.'

Lady Macbeth was angry now.

'What ghost? There's nothing there,' she told him. 'The ghost you see is like the knife you saw before you killed Duncan — it's just your fear and your imagination. There's nothing there.'

'But look at it!' her husband whispered. 'It's Banquo, can't you see?'

As Macbeth spoke, the ghost of Banquo disappeared from his sight.

'I tell you it was Banquo,' Macbeth whispered to his wife. 'I saw him there!'

'I tell you there was nothing there,' his wife whispered.

'How is it possible?' he was thinking. 'There have been terrible crimes in the past — but dead men never came back to torment their killers before!'

'Remember your guests,' Lady Macbeth warned him.

Macbeth turned to the thanes.

'Forgive me,' he said. 'It is an illness of mine. Let's eat and drink, my friends.' He took up a glass, and filled it with wine. Then he raised the glass. 'To all of us!' he cried. 'To us, and to Banquo — I wish Banquo could be here with us tonight.'

The thanes raised their glasses high in the air.

'To us and Banquo!' they cried.

At that moment Banquo's ghost came back into the room, and looked again at Macbeth.

Macbeth stared at the ghost. He was frightened.

'Why look at me?' he shouted. Now he was angry with the ghost. 'Away with you — there's nothing for you here!' He looked at his wife. 'How can you look at him, and not be afraid?' he asked. 'I am a brave man, but he frightens me.'

'What does the king mean? What is he looking at?' asked the thanes. 'What's the matter with the king?'

'It's nothing,' replied Lady Macbeth. 'It's just the king's illness. It will pass. But for now, let's part — the king needs to rest because he is ill.'

The thanes left the table. Macbeth and his wife talked together.

'Macduff didn't come tonight,' Macbeth said. 'Why do you think he didn't come?'

'I don't know,' his wife replied.

'I don't trust any of them,' Macbeth said to his wife. 'Not a single one of them. They are all my enemies. I'll go back to the three witches,' Macbeth decided. 'I must find out from them what is going to happen. Even if they tell me the worst, I must know!'

'You're tired,' Lady Macbeth told him. 'You need to sleep.'

The text and **beyond**

FCE ❶ Comprehension check

Choose the correct answer — A, B, C or D.

1 Why is Banquo unhappy?
   - A ☐ He wants to be king.
   - B ☐ He thinks that Macbeth might be a murderer.
   - C ☐ He doesn't like to be 'less than Macbeth'.
   - D ☐ He misses Duncan.

2 Macbeth is worried that
   - A ☐ Banquo's son will take his place.
   - B ☐ the thanes will find out he is a murderer.
   - C ☐ Duncan's ghost will haunt him.
   - D ☐ Banquo will become king.

3 Why does Macbeth organise a feast at the palace?
   - A ☐ He wants to celebrate becoming king.
   - B ☐ He wants to talk to Banquo about Malcolm and Donalbain.
   - C ☐ He wants to trap Banquo and his son Fleance.
   - D ☐ He wants to celebrate his friendship with Banquo.

4 Why is Macbeth so happy at the beginning of the feast?
   - A ☐ He believes that both Banquo and Fleance are dead.
   - B ☐ He's pleased to see his guests.
   - C ☐ Lady Macbeth has told him to be more cheerful.
   - D ☐ He wants to enjoy the food and wine.

5 Why does Macbeth become pale and start trembling?
   - A ☐ He is ill.
   - B ☐ He knows that Fleance is still alive.
   - C ☐ He sees the ghost of Banquo.
   - D ☐ There's nowhere for him to sit.

6 Why do the thanes leave the table?
   - A ☐ They are afraid of the ghost.
   - B ☐ They are afraid of Macbeth.
   - C ☐ They understand that Macbeth has killed Banquo.
   - D ☐ Lady Macbeth asks them to leave because the king is ill.

'You'd better go.'

We use **had better** to give advice for a specific situation.

*You**'d better** study for the test tomorrow.*   *I**'d better** not go to bed too late tonight.*

Remember that we don't use **had better** for general advice.

*You **should** always do what your parents tell you to do.* (general advice)
*You**'d better** do what your parents asked you to do.* (specific situation)

We use either **should** or **ought to** to give general advice. But we use **ought to/oughtn't to** only when we feel that it is morally right or wrong to do something.

It's going to rain. You **should** *take your umbrella.*   *He* **oughtn't to** *treat her so badly.*

2 *Had better, should* or *ought to*

Look at the following sentences, which might be said by characters in Macbeth, and decide whether it is better to use *had better, should* or *ought to*.

1   Macbeth, witches often trick people. You .... believe them.

2   The king is sacred. A thane .... always show the greatest respect for his king.

3   The witches say that Banquo's children's children will be kings. You .... keep an eye on Banquo.

4   The king is our guest. We .... kill him.

5   The important thing is that you become king. You .... worry about stupid moral questions.

6   That knife in the air was just an illusion. You .... pay any attention to it.

7   Macbeth killed the soldiers too quickly. We .... trust him.

8   Macbeth killed our father. We .... stay here any longer.

9   People will think you are mad if you talk like that. You .... keep quiet.

3 Listening

You will hear a conversation between two of the thanes who were at the feast. Before you listen, try and fill in the gaps with the words from the box. Then listen and check your answers.

> agree   Macduff   strange   think   arguing   do
> like   mad   hello   cheerful   suspects   learned

First Thane: What did you (**1**)............................ of the feast the other night?

Second Thane: It was all right at first, wasn't it? Macbeth said (**2**)............................ to everybody, and he seemed (**3**)............................ and happy.

First Thane: Then he was (**4**)............................, wasn't he? Who was he (**5**)............................ with? What did he mean when he said 'I didn't (**6**)............................ it'? I think the Queen is right. Macbeth is (**7**)............................ sometimes!

Second Thane: I don't (**8**)............................ . I don't think Macbeth is mad, exactly. It's funny [1] how he mentioned Banquo — and now we've (**9**)............................ that Banquo is dead. I don't (**10**)............................ it at all.

First Thane: You're not the only one who doesn't like it. (**11**)............................ wasn't at the feast, did you notice that? I think he (**12**)............................ Macbeth of something. A lot of people don't trust the king now.

---

1.   **funny** : (here) strange.

46

▶▶▶ **INTERNET** PROJECT ◀◀◀

Filming a ghost

With your partner discuss how you would film the banquet scene from *Macbeth*. Here are some filming terms to help you with your description.

- ▶ Close-up: filming from a short distance from the object.
- ▶ Medium shot: filming from a medium distance, from 2 to 10 metres.
- ▶ Long shot: filming from a long distance, from 10 metres or more.
- ▶ Tracking shot: filming with the camera moving (the camera can be on a cart that moves).
- ▶ Panning shot: the camera turns around but stays in the same position.
- ▶ Overhead shot: filming from above the scene.

Use these questions to help you prepare your presentation.

- ▶ Will you show the ghost of Banquo? Some of the time? Part of the time? Never?
- ▶ Will the others hear Lady Macbeth talking with Macbeth?
- ▶ How will the other people at the feast react to Macbeth's words?
- ▶ What music or other sound effects will you use?
- ▶ How will the actors be dressed? Historical costumes? Modern?

If you want to see how other people have done this scene, go to the Internet and go to www.blackcat-cideb.com or www.cideb.it. Insert the title or part of the title of the book into our search engine. Open the page to *Macbeth*. Click on the Internet project link. Scroll down the page until you find the title of this book and click on the relevant link for this project.

4 Speaking

How would you explain Macbeth's behaviour? Discuss with your partner, and then present your ideas to the class. Consider the following:

- the dagger which Macbeth saw before he killed Duncan
- the voice which he heard after he killed Duncan
- his feelings about the blood on his hands after he killed Duncan
- the ghost of Banquo which he saw at the feast

5 Summary

Number the sentences in the right order to make a summary of Parts One to Four. Then fill in the gaps with the words in the box. The first one has been done for you as an example.

> kings   frightened   castle   thanes   happy   beards   ghost   lucky
>
> drink   son   feast   witches   knife   guilty   king   enemies

A ☐ After the .... disappeared, Ross came and told Macbeth that he was the new Thane of Cawdor.
Later, when Lady Macbeth heard this, she began to plan to murder Duncan.

B ☐ But Macbeth was not happy. He remembered that Banquo too had heard the witches' predictions. Macbeth decided to have him and his .... killed. He invited them to a .... in their honour at his castle. When they were coming three of his men killed Banquo, but his son escaped.

C ☐ Her chance came when King Duncan came to stay in Macbeth's .... She gave his guards a lot to ...., and in the middle of the night Macbeth killed Duncan with the .... of one of the soldiers.

D ☐ These women, who were actually witches, told them about their future: Macbeth would become the Thane of Cawdor and then the King of Scotland; Banquo would not become so ...., but his children's children would be ....

E ☐ The next morning the murder was discovered. It appeared that the guards were ...., but Macbeth killed them both before they could speak.

F ☐ 1 Two ...., Macbeth and Banquo, had just defeated the .... of Duncan, their king.
As they were walking they saw three strange women with ....

G ☐ At the feast Macbeth tried to appear .... This became impossible when he saw something horrible: the .... of Banquo.

H ☐ The king's two sons became .... and ran away. Now they appeared guilty, and the thanes made Macbeth the new ....

Witches

There is no doubt that thunder and lightning and three witches that fly through the dirty air make a great beginning to a play. The audience's attention is immediately caught, especially since witches were, as we say now, in the news. Indeed, other writers of Shakespeare's time took advantage of the public's interest in witches and wrote plays with witches. Also, Shakespeare may have wanted to attract the attention of the King, James I, who took a great interest in witches. But we cannot say what Shakespeare himself thought.

A lot of people believed in witches in Shakespeare's time. Some thought that witches were given their power by the devil, and that they could be very dangerous. Many women were executed because they were said to be witches. At around the time that *Macbeth* was written there was a very public debate about witches in England. Reginald Scot, in his *Discovery of Witchcraft* (1584), argued that witches did not really exist. He said that the women accused of being witches were often the victims of false accusation. King James took a personal interest in the subject of witchcraft, and wrote a book on the subject, *Demonology* (1597), as a response to Scot's book. The king also tried to have all copies of Scot's book burnt. Interestingly, Scot also gave rational explanations of the supposedly miraculous magic of witches; and so his book became the first important book of magic tricks in English.

The king believed that witches existed, and secretly attended the trials of women accused of being witches. He also believed that witches had tried to destroy him and his young bride. In 1589, the arrival of James's bride, the young woman he was going to marry, Princess Anne of Denmark, was blocked by storms. James himself went to Denmark, and storms threatened his return to Scotland. The Danes began a witch-hunt to find the witches who had tried to kill James and Anne.

When James heard about these Danish witch-hunts and trials, he decided to begin his own in Scotland. Finally, a midwife [1] named Agnes Sampson was accused of being a witch and having tried to destroy the king. At first she rejected all the charges against her, but then after being tortured she confessed. One report from

---

1. **midwife** : a woman who helps women give birth to babies.

The Three Witches appearing to Macbeth and Banquo (1793) by Henry Füssli.

the period says that James did not believe she was guilty at first, but then Agnes Sampson told him the words that he and his wife had said in private on their wedding night.

During the reign of Elizabeth I and James I, the laws regarding witchcraft changed in England. Witches were no longer tried by Church courts. Witchcraft was now an ordinary crime, and was defined as 'the use, practise or exercise of any Witchcraft, Enchantment, Charm or Sorcery, whereby any person shall be killed or destroyed.' Now, someone who was found guilty of being a witch was no longer burnt: she was hanged. Also, the person who was convicted could lose his or her property to the Crown. This made it profitable for government officials to convict somebody of witchcraft and as a result the number of trials increased greatly.

James listed the main characteristics of witches:

- They are almost always women.
- They are often old.
- They have 'familiars' – animal-shaped spirits that help the witches do their magic.
- They have a 'witch's mark' or 'devil's mark' – this was supposed to be a sign made by the Devil himself on the witch to show that she belonged to him. In reality, they were any ordinary markings on the skin.
- They make models of their victims in wax and put spells on them.
- They generally live by themselves.
- They hold odd ceremonies.

It is not hard to imagine how almost any woman could be accused of being a witch. It is also not hard to imagine somebody confessing to practising witchcraft after being tortured – even if the punishment was death.

The last piece of legislation in Britain associated with witches was the Witchcraft Act of 1735. It was in force until 1951. In fact, two women, Helen Duncan and Jane Rebecca Yorke, were accused under this law in 1944. However, by 1700, the government no longer acted as if witches existed and this 1735 law did not punish people who were witches but people who pretended to be witches by calling up spirits, foretelling the future, casting spells [1] and discovering spirits. So, some people believed that the publishers of astrology columns in newspapers could be punished under the Witchcraft Act. Fortunately, in England the tragedy of witch-hunts had been transformed into the comedy of astrology.

1 Comprehension check

Say whether the following statements are true (T) or false (F), and then correct the false ones.

		T	F
1	People were not very interested in witchcraft in Shakespeare's time.	☐	☐
2	King James did not believe in witches.	☐	☐
3	Women were tortured to make them confess to being witches.	☐	☐
4	A woman believed to be witch lost her life and property.	☐	☐
5	Living alone was considered a sign that a woman was a witch.	☐	☐
6	The last two women were charged with witchcraft under English law in 1944.	☐	☐

---

1. **casting spells** : controlling people with magic.

Macbeth and the Spirits

That night the witches were in their usual place, where they were soon joined by the goddess Hecate. She was angry with them because they had spoken to Macbeth.

'You've been playing with Macbeth!' she screamed at them. 'You've been making promises to him — and he believes you. Who gave you permission to do that? Why did you do it without asking me first? You were wrong to do anything without asking me first!'

The witches were afraid of Hecate because she was very powerful.

'Listen to me,' Hecate said. 'Macbeth will come to you in the morning. He wants to know his future. This time you must do as I tell you.'

Macbeth went out in the morning to meet the three witches. When he found them they were standing over their cooking-pot. One of the witches threw a toad [1] into the pot, and they all laughed.

'A toad, yes, a toad!' the others cried. 'That's good, a toad! We'll put that in.'

Then they began to sing as they stirred [2] the contents of the pot:

1. **toad** :    2. **stirred** : mixed.

52

'Round, around, around, about, about,
Wicked staying in, good staying out.
By the feeling in my thumb
Something wicked is about to come.'

Macbeth looked at the witches with disgust.

'What are you doing?' he asked. 'What kind of magic is this?'

'We can't tell you,' one of the witches replied.

'I have come here,' Macbeth told them, 'to ask you something. You must tell me the truth!'

'Ask us your question,' the first witch said.

'We will answer,' the second witch said.

'If you don't trust us,' the third witch said, 'our masters will come to answer your question. Would you prefer that?'

'Call your masters,' commanded Macbeth. 'I want to see them. Call them for me now.'

The witches stirred their cooking-pot, and spoke some magic words. Suddenly Macbeth saw a head floating in the air in front of him. Macbeth began to speak.

'Tell me, whoever you are — '

'Don't speak!' the witches shouted. 'Listen, but don't speak. He knows what you want.'

The head began to speak:

'Macbeth, be careful of Macduff!
That is my message — it's enough.'

Then the head disappeared. The witches spoke some more magic words, and a second spirit came. The second spirit had this message for Macbeth:

'Macbeth, be brave and laugh to scorn
The power of man.
No man of woman born
Can hurt Macbeth.'

The second spirit disappeared. The witches spoke their magic words again, and a third spirit appeared. The third spirit said:

'Macbeth will never be defeated until
Birnam Wood comes to Dunsinane Hill
And fights against him.'

Macbeth considered the three messages of the spirits.

'They say that I should be careful of Macduff,' he thought. 'But Macduff is a man, and they say that no man born of woman can hurt me, so that must mean that Macduff can't hurt me! They say I can't be defeated until Birnam Wood comes to Dunsinane Hill to fight me. No one can command a wood to fight, so that must mean that I will never be defeated! These messages give me courage.'

'You have done well,' he told the witches, 'and I am happy with what you have told me. But there is one other thing I want to know. You told Banquo that his children's children would be kings — is that really true?'

When they heard this question, all the witches shouted,

'Ask no more! Ask no more!'

Macbeth became angry.

'I must have an answer!' he shouted. 'Tell me the truth — will Banquo's family be kings after me?'

The witches stopped dancing. Then they sang together:

'Show the future, break his heart,
Then we witches will depart.'

Macbeth looked, and out of the cooking-pot he saw a figure appear — it was Banquo! Then he saw a line of kings standing next to Banquo. All of the kings had the same face, and they all looked at Macbeth. Banquo smiled at Macbeth, and then he pointed at the kings. Slowly the image disappeared.

Macbeth put his head in his hands. He was in despair now. So it was true what the witches had said before, that Banquo's family would be the future kings of Scotland!

'All my crimes for nothing!' he thought. 'Banquo's family will be kings after me, and no one will remember Macbeth!'

The text and **beyond**

1 Comprehension check

The witches tell Macbeth not to speak to the spirits because

1 ☐ human beings cannot speak directly to spirits.
2 ☐ it is dangerous to speak to spirits directly.
3 ☐ they already know his thoughts.
4 ☐ Macbeth is not important enough to speak to spirits.
5 ☐ they would not answer him.

Macbeth receives four messages from the spirits. Two of the messages make him happy, and two of them make him unhappy. Which are they?

FCE 2 Sentence transformation

For questions 1-12, complete the second sentence so that it has a similar meaning to the first sentence, using the word given. Do not change the word given. You must use between two and five words, including the word given. There is an example at the beginning (0).

0 Who gave you permission to do that?
COULD
Who ...*said you could*........................... do that?

1 You must tell me the truth
NOT
You .... lies.

2 But there is one other thing I want to know.
ELSE
But there is .... I want to know.

3 No one will remember Macbeth.
WILL
Everybody .... Macbeth

4 Perhaps it was you who killed Duncan.
MIGHT
You .... Duncan.

5 The witches said I would be Thane of Cawdor.
YOU
The witches said, '..................................... Thane of Cawdor.'

6 Tonight you and Fleance will be dead.
NOT
Tonight you and Fleance .... alive.

7 All the chairs are taken

NO

There .... chairs.

8 Dead men never came back to torment their killers before.

COME

This is the first time .... to torment their killers.

9 I wish Banquo could be here with us tonight.

SORRY

I .... with us tonight.

10 I am a brave man but he frightens me.

EVEN

He .... I am a brave man.

11 'I'll go back to the three witches,' said Macbeth.

HE

Macbeth said that .... to the three witches.

12 I must find out from them what is going to happen.

ME

They .... what is going to happen.

③ Discussion

'All my crimes for nothing!' What does Macbeth mean by this?

④ Discussion

Look at the messages from the spirits again. What do *you* think they mean?

⑤ Listening

track 11

You will hear a conversation between a teacher and students. Listen carefully and decide if the statements below are true (T) or false (F).

		T	F
1	Jenny doesn't think the first message is clear.	☐	☐
2	Richard disagrees with Jenny about the first message.	☐	☐
3	Richard thinks that Macduff can't be dangerous.	☐	☐
4	Jenny thinks that the third message about Birnam Wood coming to Dunsinane Hill means that Macbeth will be defeated.	☐	☐
5	Richard thinks that the first message is the clearest.	☐	☐
6	The final message is that Banquo will become king.	☐	☐

FCE **6 The Scottish play**

For questions 1-11, read the text below about superstitions connected with
Macbeth. Use the word given in capitals at the end of the lines to form a word that
fits in the space in the same line. There is an example at the beginning (0).

Many people who work in the theatre are (0) .convinced.......... that **CONVINCE**
the play *Macbeth* brings bad luck and that you should never even
mention it by name in a theatre.

So, they often refer to as the '(1) .... Play', 'Macbee' **SCOT**
or even just 'That Play'; and they call Macbeth and Lady Macbeth
'Mr and Mrs M'.

They will tell you how (2) .... has been associated **FORTUNE**
with the play since it was first performed. They say that the
young (3) .... who was to play the part of Lady **ACT**
Macbeth (women's roles were played by men back then) in the
first (4) .... of the play caught a fever and died. **PERFORM**

It is also known that the day before his (5) .... **ASSASSINATE**
Abraham Lincoln was quoting lines from the play to some friends.

They also explain how in 1937 the (6) .... of the Old **FOUND**
Vic Theatre in London died just before that play was put on there;
and how Laurence Olivier was (7) .... killed during **NEAR**
rehearsals at the same theatre. They have many more examples
that cover more than 400 years since 'Macbee' was first
performed. These (8) .... people say that **SUPERSTITION**
Shakespeare's (9) .... of the three witches was too **REPRESENT**
precise for some real witches, who then got angry and put a curse
on the play (they didn't want their magic formulas revealed to the
general public).

(10) ...., you can fight the curse if by chance you **LUCK**
mention 'That Play' by name.

You can quote from one of Shakespeare's 'lucky' plays such as
The Merchant of Venice, or you can perform a (11) .... **COMPLICATE**
ritual involving spitting and shouting bad words.

Before you read

1 Prediction

What do you think happens next in the story?

2 Reading pictures

Look at the picture on pages 60-61 and talk about these questions.

1   Where are the people in the picture?   3   Is she trying to escape? If so, why?
2   Who's the woman with a child?   4   What are the soldiers trying to do?

Macduff

Some of the thanes of Scotland began to be suspicious of Macbeth after Banquo was murdered. They began to think that Macbeth had been involved in the death of his friend. 

'I don't think Malcolm and Donalbain paid the two soldiers to kill Duncan,' one of them said. 'They wouldn't have killed their father, because they loved him too much.'

'Why do you think they ran away then?' asked another thane.

'I think they ran away because they were frightened,' the first thane said. 'Perhaps they were frightened that someone would kill them as well.'

'What about the soldiers?' asked another thane. 'Do you really think it was them who killed the king?'

Macduff spoke next.

'I'll tell you what I think,' he said. 'I think the man who murdered Duncan wanted to become king himself,' he said. 'I think Macbeth did it.'

'And Banquo?' asked another thane. 'Who killed Banquo, I wonder? Banquo and Macbeth were good friends, weren't they?'

'I don't know about that,' Macduff said. 'But I don't feel safe here in Scotland — I'm going to England to ask the English king for help. Something is very wrong in Scotland. We live in bad times.'

Macbeth knew that the thanes were turning against him. One by one his friends abandoned him, and he felt lonely and afraid.

'I will kill all my enemies!' he decided. He thought about Macduff. 'I don't trust him,' he said to himself. 'The spirit said that Macduff was dangerous. Macduff's family will be the first to die.'

Macbeth sent some of his men to Macduff's castle. Macduff was now in

England, but Macbeth's men found Lady Macduff and her children in the castle.

'Where is your husband?' one of the men asked Lady Macduff.

'He's not here,' Lady Macduff said. 'He's gone, and you'll never find him.'

'Macduff's a traitor!' the man cried.

'You're a liar,' said the little boy. 'My father's not a traitor!'

The man took out his sword, and killed Lady Macduff and her son.

Macduff was in England at the court of the English king. Here he met Duncan's son, Malcolm. Malcolm wanted the English king to send an army into Scotland against Macbeth, and he told Macduff about the plan.

'Will you fight with us?' he asked. 'We need a man like you with the army.'

'I don't know,' Macduff said. 'It's true that Macbeth is a bad man, and a bad king — but to take an army into Scotland would be wrong. Give me time to think what I should do.'

As they were talking, Ross joined them. He had just arrived from Scotland. Malcolm was pleased to see his friend.

'What's the news from Scotland?' he asked.

'All the news is bad,' replied Ross. 'There is talk of a rebellion against Macbeth. Scotland is in danger. We need you back in Scotland, Macduff. '

'And my family?' asked Macduff. 'Is my family all right?'

'This is the worst news of all,' Ross told him. 'Macbeth's men went to your castle, and they killed your wife.'

'What about my children?' asked Macduff. 'Are my children safe?'

Ross looked very serious.

'They killed everybody,' he said. 'Your wife, your children, even the servants in the castle.'

'My children!' cried Macduff. 'My little children dead!'

'Now will you join us?' asked Malcolm. 'We're going to take an army into Scotland. Seyward will command the soldiers. We'll attack Macbeth. Think of the people he has killed — my father Duncan, Banquo, and now your family. Let's defeat him!'

'All right,' said Macduff. 'I'll come with you, but I want to be the one who kills Macbeth. I want revenge for what he did to my wife and children!'

The text and **beyond**

FCE ❶ Comprehension check

For questions 1-6, choose the correct answer — A, B, C or D.

1   Why does one of the thanes believe that Malcolm and Donalbain didn't kill Duncan?

   A ☐ They were too frightened.
   B ☐ The two soldiers killed the king.
   C ☐ They loved their father.
   D ☐ Macbeth killed the king.

2   Macduff thinks that

   A ☐ the soldiers killed Duncan because they were paid by Malcolm and Donalbain.
   B ☐ Macbeth killed Duncan because he wanted to become king.
   C ☐ Lady Macbeth killed Duncan because she wanted to help her husband.
   D ☐ Banquo killed Duncan because he wanted to become king.

3   Macduff decides to go to England because

   A ☐ he wants to find Malcolm and Donalbain.
   B ☐ he's afraid of Macbeth.
   C ☐ he doesn't want to live in Scotland while Macbeth is king.
   D ☐ he wants to ask the English king for help.

4   Macbeth decides to kill Macduff and his family because

   A ☐ he thinks Macduff is dangerous.
   B ☐ Macduff's a traitor.
   C ☐ Macduff's a liar.
   D ☐ he wants Macduff's castle.

5   At first Macduff doesn't want to fight with Malcolm against Macbeth because

   A ☐ he doesn't trust Malcolm.
   B ☐ Macbeth is a bad man.
   C ☐ he thinks it is wrong to invade his own country.
   D ☐ he wants to wait and think about it.

6   Macduff then agrees to fight because

   A ☐ he learns that Macbeth has killed his family.
   B ☐ if he defeats Macbeth he will become king.
   C ☐ he likes Malcolm.
   D ☐ Malcolm will pay him a lot of money.

2 Vocabulary

Complete the crossword puzzle. It contains words from the first six parts of the story. Some can be found in the notes, but not all of them.

Across

3 Odour.
6 Illegal and deliberate killing of a person.
8 The opposite of 'everything'.
9 Once married, a couple becomes husband and............... .
12 An area covered with trees, a small forest.
14 Awful, terrible.
15 The special chair a king sits on.
16 Plural of 'child'.
19 They went near him = They .... him.
20 Sickness.

Down

1 When you lose a war or match, you are ....
2 Unusual, odd, peculiar.
4 Surprised.
5 Somebody who is not loyal to his king is a ....
7 The nation south of Scotland.
10 Do something for or give something to somebody for his good actions or services.
11 Surprise, wonder (a noun).
13 Usually an old woman who has evil magic powers.
17 Someone who tells things which are not true.
18 Small animals like frogs (the witches like cooking them).

3 Revenge

Macduff wants revenge for the murder of his family. Discuss the following points in pairs or small groups.

1   Can you think of any novels, plays or films where characters take revenge?

2   Can you think of any real life episodes of people taking revenge?

4 Writing

Imagine you are Macduff and you have just learned the news about your family. You are now writing to your parents to tell them the terrible news. Write your letter in 120-180 words and include the following points:

- the reason why you decided to leave your family and go to England
- the news that Ross brought you
- your decision to join Malcolm and invade Scotland

Begin your letter like this:

Dear mother and father,
I am afraid I must give you some terrible news...

5 Listening

You will hear a short extract from Shakespeare's original play. Before you listen, try to fill in the gaps with words from the box. Then listen carefully and check your answers.

all   comforted   children   revenge   servants

Macduff: My (1)........................ too?

Ross: Wife, children, (2)........................, all
        that could be found.

Macduff: And I must be from thence! [1]
        My wife killed too?

Ross: I have said.

Malcolm: Be (3)........................ .
        Let's make us medicines of our great (4)........................ .
        To cure this deadly grief. [2]

Macduff: He has no children.
        All my pretty ones? Did you say (5)........................?
        O hell-kite! [3] All? What, all my pretty chickens
        And their dam [4] at one fell swoop? [5]

---

1. **And I must be from thence** : And I had to be away at the time!

2. **grief** : sadness.

3. **hell-kite** : bird from hell.

4. **dam** : mother.

5. **one fell swoop** : in one action.

The Castles of Scotland

David, Earl of Huntingdon, who became King of Scotland in 1124. From 'Ancient Armour' (1824) by Samuell Rush Meyrick.

Scotland is famous for its many beautiful castles. Some of these are still in use, and others are romantic ruins which evoke the drama and excitement of Scotland's past.

The original use of castles was military. They were the fortified homes of lords and kings. They also could be the seat of government when they belonged to the king. Also, sometimes they were defensive structures against invading armies, or they were used as military outposts by the invading army itself.

One thing is certain, there were no castles in Scotland at the time of the historical Macbeth (1005-1057). They were introduced by King David I of Scotland (1083-1153), who was the youngest son of Malcolm III (1030-1093) – this Malcolm is the son of Duncan in Shakespeare's play.

Castles came to Britain with the Norman-French invaders in 1066. Indeed, castles were a key part of their way of controlling new territories.

David first came in contact with Norman-French ways when he went to England when his sister Matilda married the Norman King of England, Henry I (1069-1135). He ended up staying in England for ten years. When he returned to Scotland, he had a Norman wife, a Norman education and English lands with Norman knights.

The Norman way of holding lands was this: a king gave his most important military men – his lords – land in exchange for military service. These lords in turn gave part of their lands to other military men, knights, also in exchange for lands. The king and all his lords and knights controlled their lands by means of castles.

So, when David came back to his native Scotland he also brought this new way of governing (which we now call feudalism), and the building of castles in Scotland began. The famous Scottish historian John of Fordun said that David was the one who built castles and towns with high towers all over Scotland.

By 1200 the king had castles all over Scotland: one in Berwick-upon-Tweed on the English border, at Ayr in the west and Dunskeath in the north. The king had all these castles because he never stayed in one place. He travelled around his kingdom. So, the king's castles also served as the centres of regional units of government, called the 'shires'.

Here are four of the most famous of Scotland's many castles.

Cawdor Castle

Cawdor Castle, which now belongs to the Earls of Cawdor, used to belong to the Thanes of Cawdor. According to legend, it was here that Macbeth murdered King Duncan.

The castle is a popular place with tourists.

Edinburgh Castle

Edinburgh castle is one of the most beautiful castles in Britain, and is visited by many tourists every year. The oldest part of the castle was built in 1130.

Balmoral Castle

Balmoral Castle was bought by Queen Victoria and her husband in 1845. Since then it has been a favourite residence for the Royal family, who usually spend their summer holidays there.

Glamis Castle

According to legend some of the scenes in Shakespeare's *Macbeth* were set here. The castle is said to contain many ghosts, and there is a mysterious locked crypt in the foundations of the building.

1 Comprehension check

Answer the following questions

1   What were castles?
2   Who introduced castles into England?
3   Who introduced castles into Scotland?
4   When did he introduce castles in Scotland?
5   Why did this person know about castles and their use?
6   What do we now call the method of government introduced by the Normans in England?
7   Why did the King of Scotland have several castles?
8   What was a 'shire'?

Before you read

track 14

① Listening

Listen to Part Seven. For questions 1-7, choose the correct answer — A, B or C.

FCE

1 The important news was that

   A ☐ Macbeth was going to invade England.

   B ☐ an army was going to invade Scotland.

   C ☐ Seyward was leading Macbeth's army.

2 It was said that the Queen

   A ☐ had her own special doctor.

   B ☐ was behaving strangely.

   C ☐ had left her husband.

3 The servant told the doctor to come because the Queen

   A ☐ talked in her sleep about the English army.

   B ☐ never slept and always walked around the castle.

   C ☐ did strange things and walked in her sleep.

4 The servant said that the Queen

   A ☐ appeared in the corridor at different times every night.

   B ☐ appeared in the corridor the same time every night.

   C ☐ never appeared in the corridor at all.

5 The Queen is obsessed by

   A ☐ Macduff's wife.

   B ☐ her dirty hands.

   C ☐ Duncan.

6 The doctor thinks that the Queen walks in her sleep because she

   A ☐ is cruel.

   B ☐ is mad.

   C ☐ is mentally ill.

7 Macbeth is ready to fight his last battle because

   A ☐ he's tired of his life.

   B ☐ he's sure he'll lose.

   C ☐ he's not afraid of his death.

The Queen

Everyone began to talk of the army that was coming from England to Scotland. Everyone knew that Seyward was leading the army. Macbeth was determined to fight his enemies, and he collected his own army.

At Macbeth's castle there were strange rumours [1] about Macbeth's Queen. Some people said the Queen had gone mad, while others said that she was very ill. There was always a doctor with her.

One day one of the Queen's servants came to the doctor.

'There is something very wrong with the Queen,' she said. 'She walks in her sleep. If you watch with me tonight, you will see something very strange.'

The doctor and the servant waited in the corridor outside the Queen's room that night.

'She will come soon,' the servant said. 'She always comes at this hour of the night. I've seen her many times.'

Just then they heard a noise from the Queen's room and the door opened. Macbeth's wife came out.

'You see,' the servant said. 'She's walking, but she's asleep.'

'But she's doing something,' the doctor said. 'She seems to be rubbing her hands.' [2]

'She always does that,' the servant told him. 'It's as if she were washing her hands. I've seen her do that before.'

The Queen began to speak to herself.

---

1. **rumours** : stories.　　2. **rubbing her hands** : moving one hand against the other.

'I'll clean these hands — I must clean these hands — Don't be afraid, Macbeth — No one will know it was us — What a lot of blood Duncan has!'

The doctor was very excited. He touched the servant's arm.

'Did you hear that?' he whispered. 'I wonder what that means.'

The Queen went on talking in her sleep.

'Macduff had a wife — Where is she now? — These hands of mine, they'll never be clean.'

'One thing is certain,' the servant said to the doctor. 'She has done terrible things, this Queen of ours.'

'I can't help her,' the doctor said. 'She is ill in the mind, and I can do nothing to help her.'

'She will soon go to bed,' the servant said.

The Queen continued to look at her hands. Then she spoke again, 'Banquo is dead — He can't hurt you — My hands! My hands — Who will wash my hands?'

Then the Queen returned to her room.

The doctor thought about what he had seen.

'It's true that she seems mad,' he thought, 'but her madness makes her tell the truth about the things she and Macbeth have done. They must have some terrible secrets!'

Macbeth waited for the enemy. Every day more of his men deserted him, but Macbeth did not care.

'Cowards! Let them go,' he thought. 'The soldiers who remain only obey me because they are frightened of me. This is the last battle I will fight. I am tired of my life. I have no friends.'

Then he remembered the words of the witches:

'No man of woman born
Can hurt Macbeth.'

'Ah!' he said to himself. 'I'm not frightened of any man — Macduff can't defeat me. What else did the witches tell me? Now I remember:

'Macbeth will never be defeated until
Birnam Wood to Dunsinane Hill
And marches against him.'

'That's it!' he thought. 'I'll take my army to Dunsinane Hill — I can't be defeated there. There is still hope. I am ready to fight now.'

The text and **beyond**

① Comprehension check

Answer the following questions.

1   What were the rumours about Macbeth's wife?

2   What did the servant ask the doctor to do?

3   Why was the Queen rubbing her hands?

4   What did the doctor think about Macbeth's wife?

5   Why did Macbeth still want to fight?

FCE ② Lady Macbeth

For questions 1-10, read the text below and think of the word which best fits each space. Use only one word in each space. There is an example at the beginning (0).

There is no doubt (**0**) .....*about*.................. it, Lady Macbeth is not a submissive woman. She (**1**) .... command and begins the series of cruel and violent murders that will take her husband to power. Even if she finally (**2**) .... mad from her feelings of guilt just as her husband has, Lady Macbeth is a formidable character. But was Shakespeare (**3**) .... against the usual views of his time regarding women? Was he trying to show that women were just as capable as men? Just as strong? It would seem almost certainly not. The idea that women and men were equal was totally unknown (**4**) .... Shakespeare's time. Instead, it was believed that God had created Adam first, and then he had created Eve (**5**) .... part of Adam's body to comfort him, to help him, to obey him - but most certainly not to rule or instigate him to power. If a woman did rule or guide her husband it meant chaos, confusion and disorder — or as we see in *Macbeth* regicide, civil war and madness.

Interestingly, Shakespeare (**6**) .... the obvious historic example of a great woman ruler, Elizabeth I, who ruled England from 1558 to 1603. But her rule as queen alone was not at all expected when she first came to the throne as a young woman. In fact, everybody expected that she (**7**) .... soon marry. So, Elizabeth and her advisors (**8**) .... to create some rather sophisticated propaganda concerning her in order for her to rule alone: Elizabeth became the 'virgin goddess'. Indeed her writers, poets and artists often (**9**) .... her to the goddess Diana or even to the Virgin Mary. This, in short, was the only way she could rule in a society that saw all women (**10**) .... either pure or impure, with nothing much in between. In short, Elizabeth skilfully avoided being seen as a kind of Lady Macbeth in the eyes of her people.

3 Iron ladies

Use the Internet or an encyclopaedia to help you match the names of these women leaders with their pictures. With your partner discuss the following questions and then present your ideas to the class:

- Do modern women rulers have to be 'virgin goddesses'?
- Do they have to present themselves as 'mothers of their countries'?
- Do you judge women leaders in the same way you judge men leaders?
- What's the public image of one of the women leaders in the pictures?
- Which one of them was known as the 'Iron Lady'?
- Which one is sometimes seen as being more capable than her famous husband?

1 Evita Peron	3 Indira Gandhi	5 Margaret Thatcher
2 Hillary Clinton	4 Mary Robinson	6 Benazir Bhutto

4 Listening

You will hear a short extract from Shakespeare's original play. Before you listen fill in the gaps with the words from the box. Then listen and check your answers.

Arabia   blood   wife   known   Heaven   hands

Lady Macbeth: The Thane of Fife had a (**1**).......................; where is she now? What, will these (**2**)...................... never be clean? No more of that, my lord, no more o' that. You mar [1] all with this starting. [2]

Doctor: Go to, [3] go to: you have (**3**)...................... what you should not.

Servant: She has spoke what she should not, I am sure of that. (**4**)...................... knows what she has known.

Lady Macbeth: Here's the smell of the (**5**)...................... still. All the perfumes of (**6**)...................... will not sweeten [4] this little hand. Oh! Oh! Oh!

FCE 5 Writing

You are the doctor who listened to Lady Macbeth while she was sleepwalking. Read part of a letter from a colleague. Write a letter giving your opinion in 120-180 words in an appropriate style.

> *What do you think about Lady Macbeth's madness?*
> *What do her words mean?*

Before you read

1 Prediction

Look at the questions below and talk about your ideas in pairs or small groups.

1 Part Eight begins like this:

Seyward's army marched steadily with Malcolm and Macduff towards Macbeth's castle.

How do you think Macbeth will react when he sees Seyward's army approach?

2 A messenger enters the room and tells Macbeth:

As I looked out towards Birnam Wood, the wood seemed to move.

What do you think the messenger means?

---

1. **mar** : ruin, destroy.
2. **starting** : surprise.
3. **Go to** : That's enough.
4. **sweeten** : make clean.

Birnam Wood to Dunsinane Hill

1 **Seyward's army marched steadily with Malcolm and Macduff towards Macbeth's castle. They stopped when they reached Birnam Wood. Malcolm was in charge of some of the soldiers, and he gave them their orders.**

'Every soldier must cut a branch from one of these trees,' he said. 'When we advance towards Dunsinane Hill, we will carry the branches in front of us. That way, no one will know how many of us there are. It will confuse Macbeth's army.'

The soldiers began to cut down branches from the trees in Birnam Wood.

2 Inside the castle Macbeth sat alone. No one wanted to be with him. Suddenly he heard a cry, and then the sound of women screaming.

A servant ran into the room.

'What is the noise?' asked Macbeth.

'The Queen is dead, sir,' the servant replied.

'She dies today,' said Macbeth. 'Today, when there is a battle to fight.' He sighed deeply. 'I don't have any time to think of her today.'

3 As Macbeth spoke, a messenger entered the room.

'Well, what is it?' asked Macbeth. 'What's the news?'

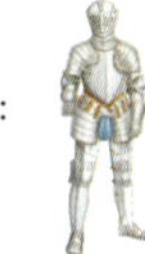

'I don't know how to tell you, sir,' the messenger said. 'I have seen something that I don't understand.'

'What did you see? Tell me quickly!' ordered Macbeth.

'I was standing on the castle wall,' said the messenger. 'As I looked out towards Birnam Wood, the wood seemed to move.'

'You're lying — it's impossible!' shouted Macbeth. Suddenly he was afraid.

'You can see for yourself, sir,' the messenger said. 'Birnam Wood is moving towards Dunsinane Hill.'

'Then I am finished,' Macbeth said to himself. 'Birnam Wood has come to Dunsinane Hill!' He thought for a moment, then he made a decision. 'If I am going to die today, I will at least die like a man. I'll die in battle.' He dressed himself in armour, [1] and went out to meet the enemy.

1. armour :

As Macbeth went out to the battle, one thought encouraged him.

'There is one hope,' he told himself. 'None of my enemies can kill me. The witches told me that I can't be killed by any man born of woman.'

Macbeth fought against the English army with courage. In the middle of the fighting Seyward's son came up to him. The young man challenged[1] him.

'Who are you?' he cried fiercely.

'You will be afraid to hear my name,' Macbeth told him. 'I am Macbeth.'

'I hate that name,' the young man told him.

'Maybe you do hate it, ' Macbeth replied. 'But you fear it, too. You are afraid of me, and you are right to be afraid of me. No one can kill me.'

'I am not afraid,' the young Seyward replied.

1. **challenged** : asked him to fight.

They took out their swords, and began to fight. Macbeth killed the young man. He looked down at the young man's body.

'You could not hurt me,' he thought. 'You were born of woman.'

5   As the battle continued, it became clear that the English army was winning. Macbeth's soldiers were killed and his castle was taken.

'What now?' he asked himself. 'My army is gone, and my castle is taken. What can I do?'

At that moment Macduff appeared.

'I have been searching for you!' he cried. 'You killed my wife and children, and now I'm going to kill you!'

Macduff raised his sword, and moved towards Macbeth.

'Keep away from me,' Macbeth warned him. 'You can't kill me. No man born of woman can kill me. Run and save yourself!'

Macduff looked at his enemy.

'Know this, Macbeth!' he shouted. 'I was not born of woman — I was taken early from my mother's womb. [1] Prepare to die!'

6   'The witches played with me!' Macbeth thought. 'Everything they said was true, but it was all a trick. I believed them, and now I am defeated.'

He turned to Macduff.

'I won't fight you,' he said.

'You must surrender then,' Macduff told him. 'You will be our prisoner, and everyone will come to mock [2] you.'

'No!' cried Macbeth. 'I won't surrender. I won't be mocked by the people. Everything is lost. Birnam Wood has come to Dunsinane Hill, and you are not of woman born. Still, I prefer to fight. If I must die, I want to die like a king.'

7   Macbeth and Macduff fought together with their swords. Macduff killed the murderer of his wife and children. He cut off Macbeth's head, and put it on the end of his sword. Then he carried it to Malcolm.

'I have brought you the traitor's head, Your Majesty,' he said. 'You will be the new King of Scotland.'

1.   **womb** [wu:m] : uterus.

2.   **mock** : make fun of.

The text and **beyond**

1 Comprehension check

Answer the following questions.

1   What did Malcolm tell the soldiers to do when the army reached Birnam Wood?
2   Why did he tell them to do this?
3   What news did the servant give Macbeth?
4   How did he react to this news?
5   Macbeth said that he has 'one hope' — what was it?
6   Who did Macbeth kill in the battle?
7   'The witches played with me!' What did Macbeth mean by this statement?
8   Why did Macbeth refuse to surrender?
9   Who becomes the new King of Scotland?

2 Listening

You will hear a short extract from the original Shakespeare's play. Before you listen try and fill in the gaps with the words from the box. Then listen and check your answers.

more   name   hell   woman   devil

afraid   fear   hateful

Macbeth: What's he
That was not born of (**1**).....................? Such a one
Am I to (**2**)....................., or none.

Young Seyward: What is thy [1] name?

Macbeth: Thou'lt [2] be (**3**)..................... to hear it.

Young Seyward: No: though thou call'st [3] thyself a hotter (**4**).....................
Than any is in (**5**)..................... .

Macbeth: My name's Macbeth.

Young Seyward: The (**6**)..................... himself could not pronounce a title [4]
More (**7**)..................... to mine [5] ear.

Macbeth: No, nor (**8**)..................... fearful. [6]

---

1. **thy** : your.
2. **thou'lt** : you will.
3. **call'st** : call.
4. **title** : name.
5. **mine** : my.
6. **fearful** : frightening.

3 Vocabulary – war

Read the definitions below and find the words. Then circle them in the word square.

The long weapon like a big knife: _ w _ _ d

Somebody captured: _ r _ _ _ _ _ r

Stop fighting and agree that you have been beaten: _ urr _ _ _ _ _

Large group of people trained to fight in wars: _ r _ y

Large building built to protect against attacks: _ _ st _ _

Walked in a military way: m _ r _ _ ed

Individual trained to fight in wars: _ o _ di _ _

When you have lost a war, you are: d _ f _ _ _ _ _

The people that you fight against in a war are your: _ n _ m _

The armed confrontation between two armies: _ _ tt _ _

When two opposing armies meet, they: f _ _ _ _

Frightened: a _ _ _ _ _

He runs away from danger: _ _ w _ _ d

D	E	F	E	A	T	E	D	H	I	S	H	A	S	T
W	A	R	B	A	T	T	L	E	P	D	S	B	O	I
U	T	E	C	I	D	O	N	T	R	C	A	R	L	S
C	A	R	N	O	E	B	E	C	I	A	U	F	D	O
A	O	A	S	E	W	E	H	E	S	I	S	I	I	N
S	G	U	F	O	M	A	D	F	O	R	I	G	E	B
T	N	D	R	R	A	Y	R	N	N	D	S	H	R	A
L	O	M	E	A	A	B	O	D	E	Y	Y	T	O	C
E	O	U	C	A	G	I	N	C	R	A	R	M	Y	K
O	S	U	N	T	O	E	D	W	H	E	N	Y	O	U
A	R	W	E	I	N	A	T	O	U	G	H	S	I	T
U	A	T	O	S	U	R	R	E	N	D	E	R	I	O
N	A	T	I	R	O	N	S	R	E	A	L	L	Y	M
E	A	N	V	E	D	R	Y	L	I	T	T	L	E	D
G	E	M	A	R	C	H	E	D	S	C	A	T	R	E

1 Discussion

A One of the themes of *Macbeth* concerns the nature of personal responsibility. Critics have argued about who is really responsible for the murder of King Duncan. Who do you think is most responsible?

THE WITCHES	They predict that Macbeth will become king. Do they make their prediction to test Macbeth?
MACBETH	He commits the murder. Would he have committed the murder without the witches? Would he have committed the murder without Lady Macbeth's encouragement?
LADY MACBETH	She knows that her husband is ambitious but that he does not want to be 'cruel'. She plans the murder of Duncan, and encourages Macbeth to carry it out.

B One of the themes of the play concerns the nature of courage. At the beginning of the play Macbeth is described as being a brave man in battle, but there are moments when he seems afraid. How does he behave in the following situations?

1 When Lady Macbeth tells him of her plan to kill Duncan?

2 Just before the murder? Just after the murder?

3 At the end of the play, when he realises that he is going to be killed?

In your opinion, what does courage consist of?

C Many critics have pointed out that the positions of Macbeth and Lady Macbeth become reversed throughout the play. Can you find evidence of this reversal of positions in what you have read? Compare the following scenes:

1 Macbeth's vision of the dagger before the murder — Lady Macbeth's vision of the blood on her hands towards the end of the play.

2 Macbeth telling his wife that he cannot kill Duncan because the king is his guest — the murder of Banquo after inviting him to the feast.

D Another of the play's themes concerns the way that Macbeth's crime isolates him from 'nature' and human affection. Can you find evidence for this gradual isolation of Macbeth in the text you have read? You may find it helpful to consider the following:

1 The relationship between Macbeth and his wife. Does this change throughout the play? Is there any sign that Macbeth keeps secrets from his wife?

2 The relationship between Macbeth and Banquo. How does this change before Banquo's murder?

3 The relationship between Macbeth and the thanes. How does this change throughout the play?

E Another of the play's themes is about the nature of remorse and conscience. Macbeth and his wife do not acknowledge their guilt in words, but both of them see or hear things that symbolise their guilt. Macbeth sees the dagger before the murder, and he hears the voice that says 'Macbeth shall sleep no more' after the murder. He also sees Banquo's ghost. Lady Macbeth sees the blood on her hands. Do you think the audience is meant to believe in the 'reality' of these phenomena, or do they have another purpose?

INTERNET PROJECT

Filming Madness

Go to the Internet and go to www.blackcat-cideb.com or www.cideb.it. Insert the title or part of the title of the book into our search engine. Open the page to *Macbeth*. Click on the Internet project link. Scroll down the page until you find the title of this book and click on the relevant link for this project.

Watch the two versions of the scene in which Lady Macbeth walks in her sleep.

Present the one you prefer to the class (you can use some of the film terms you learned on page 47).

Describe one or two improvements you would make, for example

▶ Would you show exactly what Lady Macbeth thinks she sees?

▶ Would you film Lady Macbeth only from a distance?

▶ *your own idea(s)*

The best *Macbeth* on film

The great modern poet T.S. Eliot said it was his favourite film. The famous Shakespearean critic Harold Bloom said that it is the best film version of *Macbeth*. To find out which film it is go to the Internet and go to www.blackcat-cideb.com or www.cideb.it. Insert the title or part of the title of the book into our search engine. Open the page to *Macbeth*. Click on the Internet project link. Scroll down the page until you find the title of this book and click on the relevant link for this project.

Make a short presentation of this film to your class. You can also present the trailer of this film or the death scene of Macbeth. Use these questions to help you.

1 What is the title of this film in English?
2 What does its original title mean in English?
3 Where was it made?
4 Who was its director?
5 Who played Macbeth?
6 How does this film differ from *Macbeth*?
7 How does Macbeth die in this film?

2 Picture summary

Look at these pictures from *Macbeth*. They are not in the right order. Put them in the order they appear in the play.

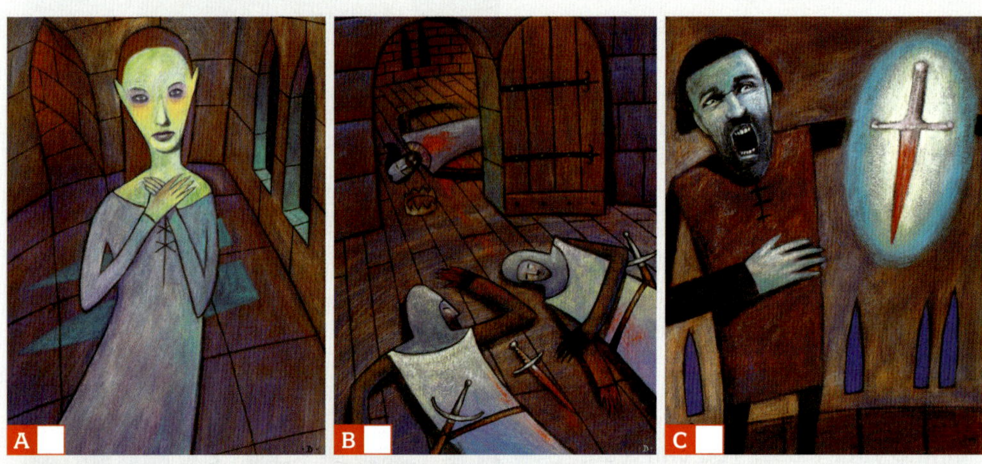

3 A graphic novel

Photocopy these two pages, cut out the pictures and stick them on paper in the right order. Think of words to put in balloons to show what the characters are speaking or thinking. Do *not* use the words that were used in this book! Then write at least a sentence under each picture to narrate what is happening.

Macbeth
Playscript

ACT ONE

It is the evening after the battle against the Thane of Cawdor and the King of Norway. Banquo and Macbeth are walking together.

BANQUO : We won, my friend. The king will be pleased with us. You were very brave today.

MACBETH : The Thane of Cawdor is defeated. We have done well.

Banquo sees the three witches. He points excitedly.

BANQUO : Look over there. Who are you? Are you women, or are you spirits?

FIRST WITCH : Welcome, Macbeth, Thane of Glamis.

MACBETH : How do you know who I am?

SECOND WITCH : Welcome, Macbeth, Thane of Cawdor.

MACBETH : Thane of Cawdor? — I'm not the Thane of Cawdor.

THIRD WITCH : Welcome, Macbeth, King of Scotland.

BANQUO : You tell my friend he will be Thane of Cawdor, and then King of Scotland. What about me? What is my future?

FIRST WITCH : You will be less than Macbeth, but more than Macbeth.

SECOND WITCH : You will be less lucky than Macbeth, but you will be more fortunate.

THIRD WITCH : You will never be king, but you will be the father of kings.

The three witches suddenly disappear.

MACBETH : How strange! They said I would be Thane of Cawdor, and then king — and you will be the father of kings! I don't know who they are, but I don't believe what they said. It makes no sense.

Ross now enters. He is looking for Macbeth.

ROSS : I have come from King Duncan. I have a message for you, Macbeth. The king is very pleased with you, and he wants to reward you. You will be the new Thane of Cawdor.

BANQUO : Thane of Cawdor!

MACBETH : The witches told the truth!

BANQUO : Be careful, my friend. Remember they also said you would be king. That's not possible. Perhaps they are bad spirits. I have heard that bad spirits try to make men do bad things by making them promises.

ACT TWO

Macbeth's castle. Lady Macbeth is reading the letter from her husband.

LADY MACBETH : 'Prepare everything for Duncan's visit. We must talk about what the witches told me. Thane of Cawdor, then King of Scotland — what can it mean?' It's a great chance for us, that's what it is. But I know you, Macbeth. You'd like to be the king, but you don't want to do anything bad. Come home, my love — I'll make you full of courage!

Macbeth's castle. Lady Macbeth is talking to her husband about Duncan's visit.

LADY MACBETH : You must act very cheerfully and innocently during the king's visit. Leave everything to me — Duncan will never leave the castle alive.

MACBETH : We cannot kill the king! He's been a good friend to me, and I can't murder him.

LADY MACBETH : Why did you tell me about the three witches, then? Don't you want to be king? Are you just frightened? Be brave, and you can have the throne!

MACBETH : But if we fail? What happens to us if we fail?

LADY MACBETH : Don't worry about that. We won't fail. I've got a plan. Duncan's room is guarded by two soldiers. I'll make sure that they drink a lot of wine. They won't know what's happening. It will be easy for you to go into the king's room and kill him. We can blame the soldiers for the murder.

MACBETH : You're right! No one will think it was us.

It is late at night in the castle. Macbeth comes out of the two soldiers' room. He is holding a knife, and his hands are covered in blood. He looks frightened. Lady Macbeth is waiting for him.

LADY MACBETH : Well? Did you do it?

MACBETH : Duncan is dead. I have done a terrible thing. Afterwards, I heard a voice. It said, 'There will be no more sleep. Macbeth has murdered sleep'. It was a frightening voice.

LADY MACBETH : Did it say anything else?

MACBETH : Yes. It cried out, 'Macbeth has murdered sleep — Macbeth will never sleep again'. It was a loud voice. I thought everyone in the castle would hear it.

LADY MACBETH : You're like a child! There was no voice, it was just your fear you heard. But the knife — why are you still carrying the knife? Go and put it in the soldiers' room!

MACBETH : I can't go back in there — I'll never go back in there!

LADY MACBETH : Give the knife to me. I'm not afraid. I'll put it in the soldiers' room.

Lady Macbeth goes into the soldiers' room. Macbeth is alone. He is looking at the blood on his hands.

MACBETH : I have done a terrible thing. This blood will never go away. I wish I hadn't done it!

Lady Macbeth comes back from the soldiers' room. Her hands are covered with blood.

LADY MACBETH : Look at my hands. They're red like yours — but I'm not afraid like you! A little water will remove the traces of our crime.

ACT **THREE**

Macduff and Lennox have just entered the castle. It is very early in the morning. They have made a noise, and woken up the porter. Macbeth comes down to see what is happening.

MACDUFF : Did you go to bed late, my friend? Perhaps you drank too much before you went to bed. Is that why you didn't hear the knocking on the gate?

PORTER : It's true, sir. I did drink too much last night.

MACDUFF : Good morning, Macbeth. Is the king awake yet?

MACBETH : He's still sleeping. Shall I wake him for you?

MACDUFF : I'll wake him myself. He asked me to come early this morning.

Macduff goes to the king's room. Macbeth and Lennox talk.

LENNOX : What a terrible night! The wind blew fiercely all night. Our chimneys were blown down. Some people said that they heard horrible screams.

MACBETH : It was just bad weather. It didn't mean anything.

They hear Macduff shouting from the king's room.

LENNOX : What is it? What's the matter? Is it the king?

Macduff comes from the king's room.

MACDUFF : It's dreadful, too dreadful. Go and look for yourselves.

MACBETH : Come on!

Macbeth and Lennox run off to the king's room.

MACDUFF : Murder! Murder! Sound the alarm!

People come from everywhere when they hear the shouting and the alarm. Enter Lady Macbeth, Malcolm and Donalbain. Macduff goes up to Malcolm and Donalbain.

LADY MACBETH : What is it? Why is there such a noise?

MACDUFF : There is terrible news.

MALCOLM : Tell us. Is it the king?

DONALBAIN : What about our father?

MACDUFF : He's been murdered!

Macbeth and Lennox come down from the king's room.

MACBETH : It's true — Duncan has been murdered.

MALCOLM : Who did it? Who killed the king?

LENNOX : It was the two soldiers. When we went into their room, they were sleeping. They were covered in blood. We asked them questions, but they couldn't answer. It must have been them who killed Duncan.

MACDUFF : But why? Why would they do it? We must ask them why.

MACBETH : We can't ask them anything. When I saw them covered in the king's blood I killed them. I'm sorry. I shouldn't have done it. But I loved the king.

MACDUFF : Now we'll never know why they did it, or if someone paid them to do the murder.

LADY MACBETH : Oh, the king! The poor king! What a terrible thing to happen here, in my house. Who could have done it?

Lady Macbeth falls to the floor.

MACDUFF : The shock is too great for her. Help her, someone.

Macbeth picks up his wife, and helps her away.

BANQUO : Let's meet back here in one hour — we need to plan what to do about the king's murder.

Everybody leaves, except Malcolm and Donalbain.

DONALBAIN : I don't feel safe here. Someone has murdered our father, and I don't believe what Macbeth told us.

MALCOLM : I don't believe Macbeth, either. Why would the two soldiers kill the king? It doesn't make any sense. We'll never really know what happened.

DONALBAIN : Macbeth killed them too quickly.

MALCOLM : What do you mean?

DONALBAIN : Macbeth said he killed the soldiers because he was angry. I don't think he was angry — I think he killed them because he didn't want them to be able to answer our questions!

MALCOLM : You suspect Macbeth?

DONALBAIN : I don't know. But I think we should get away from this castle. Whoever killed our father is still here — and he may try to kill us next.

MALCOLM : I agree. I'll go to England. I've got friends there.

DONALBAIN : And I'll go to Ireland.

Malcolm and Donalbain leave. Banquo, Macduff and the others come back.

MACDUFF : It must have been Malcolm and Donalbain who killed Duncan. They've run away from the castle. I think I know what happened. They paid the two soldiers to kill the king. They wanted the throne for themselves. We must make sure they suffer for this terrible crime!

BANQUO : Who shall we have as the new king?

MACDUFF AND THE OTHERS : Macbeth! Let's make Macbeth the new king! He was Duncan's friend.

ACT **FOUR**

MACBETH : There is a feast tonight at the castle. You will be the guest of honour, my friend.

BANQUO : I will be there.

MACBETH : Bring your son Fleance with you — he's invited as well.

BANQUO : We will both be there. We are riding out this afternoon, but we will be at the castle tonight for the feast.

MACBETH : Tomorrow we must talk. I hear that Malcolm and Donalbain have gone to England and Ireland. They are trying to make trouble for me. We must decide what to do about them.

Banquo goes away, and Lady Macbeth joins Macbeth.

LADY MACBETH : You never seem happy, my love.

MACBETH : I am worried — I have enemies, you know.

LADY MACBETH : Tonight you must try to be cheerful at the feast. Remember that!

MACBETH : Tonight I will be cheerful, I promise.

LADY MACBETH : Forget the past. What we did, we did. We can't change anything now.

MACBETH : Sometimes I worry about Banquo and Fleance. I don't feel safe when I think of them.

LADY MACBETH : What can we do about them?

MACBETH : I have already done something — it's better that you don't know the details!

Outside the castle that evening. Three men are hiding in the darkness.

FIRST MURDERER : Are you sure Banquo and Fleance will come this way?

SECOND MURDERER : They'll come this way.

THIRD MURDERER : And when they do, we'll kill them both. Macbeth wants them to die.

FIRST MURDERER : Here they are! I can hear them.

Banquo and Fleance enter. The murderers attack Banquo.

THIRD MURDERER : Now!

SECOND MURDERER : Attack!

BANQUO : Ride, Fleance, ride! It's a trap!

Macbeth's castle, at the feast.

MACBETH : Welcome — I'm happy to see you all. Tonight we will enjoy ourselves with food and wine.

Enter the first murderer. Macbeth approaches him.

MACBETH : Well? How did it go?

FIRST MURDERER : Banquo is dead.

MACBETH : And Fleance? Tell me that Fleance is dead as well!

FIRST MURDERER : Fleance escaped us. He is free.

MACBETH : Then I'm not safe, after all. Go — there is blood on your face. We'll talk tomorrow.

LENNOX : Will Your Majesty sit with us?

MACBETH : Where shall I sit? All the chairs are taken.

LENNOX : There is an empty chair next to me.

Macbeth looks at the chair indicated by Lennox. He sees Banquo's ghost in the chair.

MACBETH : I didn't do it! Don't look at me like that. I didn't do it!

LENNOX : What's the matter with the king? Who is he talking to — that chair's empty!

LADY MACBETH : It is an illness of his. It will soon pass.

LADY MACBETH (to her husband) : What's the matter with you? Remember your guests. Where's your courage?

MACBETH (to his wife) : My courage! I'm a brave man to look at that ghost, and not run away!

LADY MACBETH (to her husband) : What ghost? There's nothing there. This ghost you see is like the knife you saw before you killed Duncan. It's your fear and your imagination.

MACBETH : But look at it! It's Banquo, can't you see?

The ghost disappears. Macbeth speaks to the guests.

MACBETH : Forgive me. It is an illness of mine. Let's drink to us. To us and to Banquo!

THE GUESTS : To us and to Banquo!

The ghost comes back into the room.

MACBETH : Why look at me? Away with you! Leave me alone!

THE GUESTS: What does the king mean? What is he looking at? What's wrong with him?

LADY MACBETH : The king is ill. He needs to rest.

The guests leave the room. Lady Macbeth and Macbeth are alone.

MACBETH : Macduff didn't come tonight. Why didn't he come?

LADY MACBETH : I don't know.

MACBETH : I don't trust any of them. They're all my enemies. I'll go back to the three witches. I must find out from them what is going to happen. Even if they tell me the worst, I must know!

ACT **FIVE**

Macbeth with the three witches.

MACBETH : I have come here to ask you something. You must tell me the truth.

THIRD WITCH : If you don't trust us, our masters will come to answer your question. Would you prefer that?

MACBETH : Call your masters. I want to see them. Call them now.

The witches stir the contents of the cooking-pot. A head rises in the air in front of Macbeth.

MACBETH : Tell me —

THE WITCHES : Don't speak! He knows what you want.

THE HEAD : Macbeth, be careful of Macduff! That's my message, it's enough.

The head disappears. The witches stir the contents of the pot again, and a second spirit appears.

SECOND SPIRIT : Macbeth, be brave and laugh to scorn the power of man. No man of woman born can hurt Macbeth.

The second spirit disappears. The witches stir the pot once again, and a third spirit appears.

THIRD SPIRIT : Macbeth will never be defeated until Birnam Wood to Dunsinane Hill fights against him.

The third spirit disappears.

MACBETH : You have done well. But there is one thing more that I want to know. Will Banquo really be the father of kings?

ALL THE WITCHES : Ask no more! Ask no more!

MACBETH : I must have an answer — tell me the truth!

ALL THE WITCHES : Show the truth, and break his heart. Then we witches will depart.

The ghost of Banquo appears in front of Macbeth. He is surrounded by kings. The image stays for a moment, and then disappears. Macbeth puts his head in his hands. He is in despair.

ACT **SIX**

Two thanes are talking with Macduff about Macbeth.

FIRST THANE : I don't think Malcolm and Donalbain paid the two soldiers to kill their father. They loved him too much.

SECOND THANE : Why did they run away, then?

FIRST THANE : I think they were frightened.

SECOND THANE : What about the soldiers? Do you think they killed Duncan?

MACDUFF : I'll tell you what I think. I think the man who killed Duncan wanted to be king himself.

FIRST THANE : And Banquo? Who killed Banquo, I wonder? Do you think it was Macbeth?

MACDUFF : I don't know. But I don't feel safe here in Scotland. I'm going to England. Something is wrong in Scotland. We live in bad times.

England. Malcolm is trying to persuade Macduff to fight against Macbeth.

MALCOLM : Will you fight with us? We need a man like you.

MACDUFF : I don't know. It's true that Macbeth is a bad man — but I am not a traitor. Give me time to think about it.

Enter Ross.

MACDUFF : What's the news from Scotland?

ROSS : All the news from Scotland is bad. There is talk of a rebellion against Macbeth. We need you, Macduff.

MACDUFF : And my family — is my family all right?

ROSS : This is the worst news of all. Macbeth sent some men to your castle. They killed your wife.

MACDUFF : What about my children? Are my children safe?

ROSS : They killed everybody — your wife, your children, even the servants in the castle.

MACDUFF : Not my children! My little children dead!

MALCOLM : Now will you join us against Macbeth? We'll take an army into Scotland. We'll defeat Macbeth!

MACDUFF : I'll come with you. I want to be the man who kills Macbeth — I want revenge!

ACT **SEVEN**

Macbeth's castle. A woman servant is talking to Lady Macbeth's doctor.

SERVANT : There is something very wrong with the Queen. She walks in her sleep at night. I want you to watch with me tonight, to see what happens.

DOCTOR : The Queen appears.

SERVANT : There she is! She's walking, but she's asleep.

DOCTOR : What's she doing? She seems to be rubbing her hands.

SERVANT : She always does that. Is she washing her hands?

The Queen begins to speak to herself.

LADY MACBETH : I'll clean these hands — I must clean these hands — Don't be afraid, Macbeth — No one will know it was us — What a lot of blood Duncan has!

DOCTOR : Did you hear that? I wonder what it means.

LADY MACBETH : Macduff had a wife — Where is she now? — These hands of mine, they'll never be clean.

DOCTOR : I can't help her — she's mad.

LADY MACBETH : Banquo is dead — he can't hurt you — My hands! — Who will wash my hands?

SERVANT : She will soon go to bed.

DOCTOR : She is mad, but her madness tells the truth. Macbeth and his wife have done some terrible things. I wish I was away from this castle!

ACT **EIGHT**

Seyward's army has arrived at Birnam Wood.

MALCOLM : Every soldier must cut a branch from one of these trees. We'll carry the branches in front of us, it will confuse Macbeth's army.

Inside Macbeth's castle. Macbeth with a servant.

MACBETH : What is the noise?

SERVANT : The Queen is dead, sir.

MACBETH : She dies today, when there is a battle to fight. I cannot think of her today.

A messenger enters the room.

MACBETH : Well, what is it? What's the news?

MESSENGER : I don't know how to tell you, sir. I have seen something that I don't understand.

MACBETH : What did you see? Tell me quickly.

MESSENGER : As I looked out towards Birnam Wood, the wood seemed to move.

MACBETH : You're lying — it's impossible!

MESSENGER : You can see for yourself, sir. Birnam Wood is moving towards Dunsinane Hill.

MACBETH : Then I am finished. Birnam Wood has come to Dunsinane Hill! But I will die like a man. Anyway, no man of woman born can kill me — it's my one hope.

The battle. Young Seyward sees Macbeth.

YOUNG SEYWARD : Who are you?

MACBETH : You will be afraid to hear my name. I am Macbeth.

YOUNG SEYWARD : I hate that name!

MACBETH : You fear it, too.

YOUNG SEYWARD : I am not afraid.

Macbeth and Young Seyward fight — Seyward is killed. Macduff approaches Macbeth.

MACDUFF : I have been searching for you. Today I will kill you!

MACBETH : Keep away from me! You can't kill me. No man born of woman can kill me. Run, and save yourself.

MACDUFF : Know this, Macbeth. I was not born of woman. I was taken early from my mother's womb. I'll kill you for the deaths of my wife and children.

MACBETH : I won't fight you!

MACDUFF : You must surrender, then. You will be our prisoner. Everyone will come to mock you.

MACBETH : No! I won't surrender. I won't be mocked by the people. Everything is lost. Birnam Wood has come to Dunsinane Hill, and you are not of woman born. Still, I prefer to fight.

Macbeth and Macduff fight. Macbeth is killed.

This reader uses the **EXPANSIVE READING** approach, where the text becomes a springboard to improve language skills and to explore historical background, cultural connections and other topics suggested by the text.

The new structures introduced in this step of our **READING & TRAINING** series are listed below. Naturally, structures from lower steps are included too. For a complete list of structures used over all the six steps, see *The Black Cat Guide to Graded Readers*, which is also downloadable at no cost from our website, blackcat-cideb.com.

The vocabulary used at each step is carefully checked against vocabulary lists used for internationally recognised examinations.

Step **Four B2.1**

All the structures used in the previous levels, plus the following:

Verb tenses
Present Perfect Simple: *the first / second* etc. *time that ...*
Present Perfect Continuous: unfinished past with *for* or *since* (duration form)

Verb forms and patterns
Passive forms: Present Perfect Simple
Reported speech introduced by precise reporting verbs (e.g. *suggest, promise, apologise*)

Modal verbs
Be / get used to + *-ing*: habit formation
Had better: duty and warning

Types of clause
3rd Conditional: *if* + Past Perfect, *would(n't) have*
Conditionals with *may / might*
Non-defining relative clauses with: *which, whose*
Clauses of concession: *even though*; *in spite of*; *despite*

Available at Step **Four**:

- **American Horror** Edgar Allan Poe
- **Beowulf**
- **The Big Mistake and Other Stories** Nella Burnett-Stuart and Bruna Deriu
- **The Canterbury Tales** Geoffrey Chaucer
- **A Christmas Carol** Charles Dickens
- **Daisy Miller** Henry James
- **Dracula** Bram Stoker
- **Famous British Criminals from The Newgate Calendar**
- **The House of the Seven Gables** Nathaniel Hawthorne
- **Jack the Ripper** Peter Foreman
- **The Last of the Mohicans** James Fenimore Cooper
- **Moby Dick** Herman Melville
- **The Moonstone** Wilkie Collins
- **Le Morte d'Arthur** Sir Thomas Malory
- **The Secret Agent** Joseph Conrad
- **The Sign of Four** Sir Arthur Conan Doyle
- **A Study in Scarlet** Sir Arthur Conan Doyle
- **Tom Jones** Henry Fielding
- **The Tragedy of Dr Faustus** Christopher Marlowe
- **The Turn of the Screw** Henry James
- **The Valley of Fear** Sir Arthur Conan Doyle
- **Washington Square** Henry James
- **Wicked and Humorous Tales** Saki
- **The Woman in White** Wilkie Collins

READING SHAKESPEARE

- **Macbeth**
- **The Merchant of Venice**
- **A Midsummer Night's Dream**
- **Much Ado About Nothing**
- **Othello**